The Liberty and Ormond Boys

Maynooth Studies in Local History

SERIES EDITOR Raymond Gillespie

This is one of six short books published in the Maynooth Studies in Local History series in 2005. Like their predecessors they are, in the main, drawn from theses presented for the MA course in local history at NUI Maynooth. Also, like their predecessors, they range widely over the local experience in the Irish past. That local experience is presented in the context of the complex social and political world of which it is part, from the great houses of Armagh to the rural housing of Leitrim and from the property developers of eighteenth-century Dublin to those who rioted on the streets of the capital. The local experience cannot be a simple chronicling of events relating to an area within administrative or geographically-determined boundaries since understanding the local world presents much more complex challenges for the historian. It is an investigation of the socially diverse worlds of poor and rich. It explores the lives of those who joined the British army in the First World War as well as those who, on principle, chose not to do so. Reconstructing such diverse local worlds relies on understanding what the people of the different communities that made up the localities of Ireland had in common and what drove them apart. Understanding the assumptions, often unspoken, around which these local societies operated is the key to recreating the world of the Irish past and gaining insight into how the people who inhabited those worlds lived their daily lives. As such, studies such as those presented in these short books, together with their predecessors, are at the forefront of Irish historical research and represent some of the most innovative and exciting work being undertaken in Irish history today. They also provide models that others can follow and adapt in their own studies of the Irish past. In such ways can we better understand the regional diversity of Ireland and the social and cultural basis of that diversity. If these books also convey something of the vibrancy and excitement of the world of Irish local history today they will have achieved at least some of their purpose.

Maynooth Studies in Local History: Number 64

The Liberty and Ormond Boys
Factional riot in eighteenth-century Dublin

James Kelly

FOUR COURTS PRESS

Set in 10pt on 12pt Bembo by
Carrigboy Typesetting Services, County Cork for
FOUR COURTS PRESS LTD
7 Malpas Street, Dublin 8, Ireland
e-mail: info@four-courts-press.ie
http://www.four-courts-press.ie
and in North America for
FOUR COURTS PRESS
c/o ISBS, 920 N.E. 58th Avenue, Suite 300, Portland, OR 97213.

ISBN 1–85182–897–4

Printed in Ireland by
ßetaprint Ltd, Dublin

Contents

	Acknowledgments	6
	Introduction	7
1	The Kevan Bail and the commencement of factional disorder	14
2	The Ormond and Liberty Boys, 1730–70	27
3	The changing character of factional riot, 1770–91	45
	Conclusion	51
	Notes	53

FIGURES

1	Dublin c.1756 after John Rocque	8
2	Map of Oxmantown and Smithfield, by John Rocque, 1756	15
3	Map of Ormond Market and Ormond Quay, by John Rocque, 1756	17
4	Map of Kevan's Port, Long Lane and environs, by John Rocque, 1756	23
5	Map of Newmarket, Weaver's Square, Dolphin's Barn areas, by John Rocque, 1756	43

Acknowledgments

I wish to thank Prof. Raymond Gillespie for the invitation to prepare this study for the Maynooth Studies in Local History; it is a pleasure to be part of a series with which I have had close contact as external examiner of the programme for local history at NUI, Maynooth. A shorter version of the work offered here was delivered as the Presidential Address to the Irish Historical Society in December 2003, and I would like to thank the Society, and the audience for their comments and observations.

Most of the research that has gone to this work was conducted in the National Library of Ireland and the Cregan Library, St Patrick's College; it is a pleasure to acknowledge the support and assistance of the staffs of both institutions and of the other record repositories and libraries, notably Trinity College Dublin, the National Archives of Ireland and the Public Record Office of Northern Ireland, that have facilitated the completion of this study. I wish also to thank Marian Lyons for her helpful comments on the text and Dr Matthew Stout for his cartographic assistance. I am grateful to my departmental colleagues, Diarmaid Ferriter, Carla King, Dáire Keogh, Marian Lyons and Matthew Stout, for their continuing fellowship and support.

Introduction

It is widely assumed that 'faction fighting', as the ritualised violent exchanges involving large local groups is known in Ireland, was confined in time to the 19th century and in space to the countryside.[1] Neither claim is sustainable. Factional motivated disorder, while commonplace in the countryside during the 19th century, emerged as an identifiable social phenomenon during the previous century, and while the more remote forces that facilitated its generation may lie still deeper, it first attained a sufficiently distinctive form then to generate an evidential legacy that permits the identification of its major features. Significantly, and in this it bears comparison with the practice of abducting women of fortune,[2] whereas those who engaged in faction fighting in the 19th century were 'country people', factional activity in the 18th century not only possessed a distinct urban dimension, it was more structured and developed in that environment than it was in its rural setting, though such claims must be treated with a measure of scepticism pending more detailed enquiry. Indeed, compared with 18th-century agrarian protest, the main manifestations of which have been thoroughly explored,[3] factional disorder has attracted little attention. It has not passed entirely unnoticed; the notoriety of the Ormond and Liberty Boys – the most enduring factions active in Dublin – has ensured them frequent passing mention. But though Sean Murphy has perceptively explored their impact during the 1740s, and Patrick Fagan has established the existence in the late 1720s and early 1730s of the faction known as the Kevan (or Cavan) Bail, the nature, extent and response to faction remains opaque.[4] There is no agreement furthermore on its purpose, as Murphy's hypothesis that 'the violence and persistence of the Liberty and Ormond feud were such that it must have had more to it than mere ritual faction fighting' and that it may have echoed the 'politico-religious sectarian disturbances in early 18th-century Dublin' has been explicitly rejected by Fagan, who has concluded that 'the main cause of the feud' in which they engaged 'can be boiled down ... to a simple case of two rival gangs of hooligans spoiling for a fight'.[5]

The latter observation begs more questions than it answers, but whereas the student of 19th-century rural faction can draw on a large volume of responsive source material to assist with the reconstruction of the phenomenon, the leaner evidential seam for urban faction in the 18th century is tangibly less forthcoming.[6] There is a small number of influential descriptions, purportedly

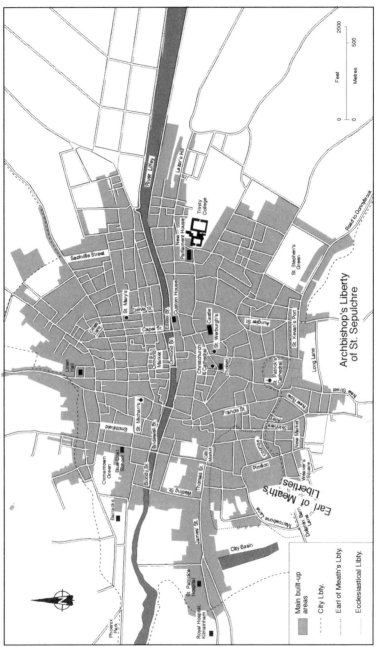

1 Dublin *c*.1756 after John Rocque

informed by personal observation, of which that penned in the 1840s by John Edward Walsh in his serendipitous excursus into the Georgian under-belly, *Ireland sixty years ago*, is the best known. Written in a racy style, comparable to Jonah Barrington's better known reminiscences of the excesses of the Georgian gentry, Walsh's account of the Liberty and Ormond Boys offers an arresting description of factionalised feuding 'among the lower orders' in Dublin. However, it is fundamentally ahistorical in not locating them within a secure chronological frame of reference; misleading in that it relies for its basic narrative on the brief surge of disorder per-petrated by aggrieved textile operatives during the difficult early 1790s when the social memory of the activities of the Liberty and Ormond Boys was beginning to fade; and, therefore, inaccurate in its identification of the quays and the Liffey bridges as their battleground; exaggerated in its assessment of their impact on commercial activity; and misleading in implying that the authorities were powerless to prevent the disruption of quotidian activity in the city. The following extract is indicative of Walsh's seductive style and deceptively authoritative approach:

> A feud and deadly hostility had grown up between the Liberty boys, or tailors and weavers of the Coombe, and the Ormond boys, or butchers who lived in Ormond-market, … which caused frequent conflicts; and it is the memory of many now living that the streets, and particularly the quays and bridges, were impassable in consequence of the battles of these parties. The weavers descending from the upper regions beyond Thomas-street, poured down on their opponents below; they were opposed by the butchers, and a contest commenced on the quays which extended from Essex to Island Bridge. The shops were closed; all business suspended; the sober and peaceable compelled to keep [to] their houses; and those whose occasions led them through the streets where the belligerents were engaged, were stopped; while the war of stones and other missiles was carried on across the river, and the bridges were taken and retaken by the hostile parties … For whole days the intercourse of the city was interrupted by the feuds of these factions …[7]

In view of the limitations of the recollections upon which Walsh's narrative depends, and the unavailability of the court transcripts, constabulary and magistrate's reports, and parliamentary enquiries (such as supply rich detail on the extent, nature and conduct of rural faction in the 19th century), one is obliged to look elsewhere for usable contemporary evidence, and, as the investigations of agrarian discontent have repeatedly demonstrated, the most consistently rewarding is the contemporary press.[8]

Newspapers are not an unproblematical evidential source, because they invariably reflected the hostile attitude of respectable society to the factional activities they were reporting. Moreover, the limited space allocated to local and domestic news combined with the summary style of presentation that was favoured encouraged the publication of terse reports, in the manner of that offered by the *Dublin Weekly Journal* on 17 September 1748, that '[On] Sunday last, there was a riot *as usual* between the Ormond and Liberty Boys, in which several were wounded on both sides'.[9] Individually, reports of this ilk are of limited worth in reconstructing the world of faction, but they are not representative of the full corpus of evidence, and their value is enhanced when combined with other reports, which provide the names and places of origin of participating factions, the dates and locations of riots, estimates of the number of participants, the injuries inflicted, the weapons used, and so on. In addition, the existence of faction did not pass unnoticed by the authorities, civil and religious, and the employment of an extensive range of official and institutional pronouncements and contextual descriptions permits a recon-struction of the lineaments of the world of faction in 18th-century Dublin that is revealing both of the activities of individual factions, and of the wider phenomenon of factional violence in 18th-century Dublin.

Information from these sources certainly serves to correct the further misimpression conveyed by J.R. Walsh that factional disorder in the 18th century was confined to Dublin. Pending a specific enquiry into its spatial distribution, any attempt to correct this must be tentative, but reports of factional activity in urban centres other than Dublin and at patterns and fairs in a variety of rural locations indicate that the culture of faction fighting that obtained in 18th-century Dublin was part of a national phenomenon. It was not equally prevalent in all part of the country, but reports of factional activity, sometimes involving many hundreds of people, at Portumna, Co. Galway, and Beltra, Co. Sligo, in Connacht; on the banks of the Lagan Canal, Co. Down; Mullingar and Kilcock in the north midlands; Kilcavan, Co. Wicklow; Killaloe, Co. Clare; Clonmel, Co. Tipperary; Urlingford, Co. Kilkenny, and Ring in west Co. Cork provide an indication of its geo-graphical range.[10] Significantly, based on the concentration of reports from factional activity in Cos. Cork, Clare, Limerick, Tipperary, Kilkenny, Queen's and Carlow, its rural heartland coincided with that of agrarian protest in Munster and south Leinster. Equally significantly, it was not confined in its urban manifestation to the fast growing conurbation of Dublin. Reports attesting to the existence in Limerick city in the 1779 of the 'Garrison Boys', and the propensity of the County of Limerick Boys to engage each Easter at Thomond Gate with the County Clare Boys during the 1770s and 1780s suggest that the factional impulse was strong in that city.[11] It was stronger still in Cork city, which rivalled Dublin in sustaining a number of factional groups (the Blackpool, Fair Lane and Blarney Lane Boys) over an extended length of time. Active between the early 1750s, from when the initial record of their engagement in a trial of strength to determine which would 'bring home' the May bush dates, and the late 1770s, when the focus of factional activity in the region moved to Cork county, the fact that these factions attracted audiences 'to the number of two thousand and upwards' to view their encounters, which took place weekly in the early 1770s, is equally revealing of their popular appeal as well as of the incapacity of the authorities to deter them from the 'barbarous and savage custom of fighting'.[12] This mirrored the situation in Dublin, and a further connection can be made with the capital in that butchers and weavers constituted the main employments of the major factions in both. However, by comparison with Dublin, factional activity in Cork was limited and short-lived, and since none of the Cork factions have left more than a faint impression on the surviving record, it is to Dublin and to the factional behaviour that can be identified there that one must turn in an first instance in order to establish the character and trajectory of urban factionalism in 18th-century Ireland.

A number of major economic and social phenomena were crucial to the creation of the circumstances conductive to the emergence of a strong factional impulse in Dublin. The first of these was the rapid physical and demographic growth the city experienced between the mid-17th and mid-18th centuries, because this resulted in the emergence of a number of densely populated artisan areas that sustained urban faction. The parallel decline of the guilds was no less crucial, since the fast-changing economic environment of the early 18th century undermined the venerable, and inherently socially stabilising, practice whereby craftsmen graduated from apprentice to journeyman to master. As a result, journeymen and apprentices were less bound by the traditional disciplines of the guild system and increasingly disposed to participate in other forms of associative activity of which the combination is the best known, but faction represented another outlet. Thirdly, the 18th century also witnessed changes in the pattern of recreational activity as the combination of rapid urban growth, and the diminishing capacity of the traditional guardians of behaviour – family and social networks with deep roots in long-established areas, the guilds and the churches – to regulate the activities of young men, permitted the latter to ventilate their energies in a more rambunctious and violent fashion. None of these forces operated in isolation from the wider economic and political environment, of course. Indeed, in a world in which both newly-formed and entrenched atavistic animosities encouraged violent disorder, and in which the vulnerability of the population to distress when weather patterns were adverse and the international commercial climate unfavourable legitimated public protest, the political, social, demographic and economic environments each contributed to the emergence of definable factional interests committed to the expression of local and sectoral identities through the language of violence.

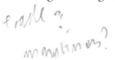

The process whereby this resulted in the emergence of named factions was sufficiently well advanced in Dublin by the 1720s for the first manifestations of faction to be detectible, though it was not until the end of the decade that the city first named faction – the Kevan or Cavan Bail – assumed an identifiable organisational form. Obliged to contend during the 1730s with a number of rivals, of which the bodies that became the Ormond and Liberty Boys are but the best known, the level of violence appealed to when these factions clashed was measured. Fatalities were not unusual, but the limited violence to which the protagonists had recourse was consistent with the character of a factional culture; that is, fighting was a test of strength and not *per se* a life or death struggle, and it was resorted to in order to establish which of two contending and antipathetic factional interests was the stronger. To this end, it was crucial to the reputation of a faction that it was capable of defending its own distinct space or, when fighting took place on neutral territory, that it refused to yield to its antagonist. This made little sense to contemporaries who did not share the factional impulse, but it effectively decodes the bemused observation of J.D. Herbert in respect of the Ormond and Liberty Boys that 'they could give no good reason for their abominable destructive aversion to each other, but that the Ormond should not subdue the Liberty, and *vice versa* with the other party'.[13] While it is apparent why a faction should seek at all costs to avoid the humiliation and the implications of sub-ordination inherent in its defeat in a 'fight' with a rival, territorial supremacy also featured prominently among their *raisons d'être*. Thus, the contests associated with 'bringing home ... May bushes' involving the Blackpool, Fair Lane and Blarney Lane Boys in Cork in the 1760s and 1770s, depicted by some contemporaries reductively as 'fighting about May-poles', was also a symbolic struggle for territorial control and domination.[14]

Since they neither comprehended nor had any sympathy with what seemed to them wanton and motiveless riotousness, the authorities sought unhesitantly to put an end to faction fighting, and their interventions were generally sufficient to disrupt, and frequently to halt the pattern of factional violence. They were unable to eradicate the impulse that fuelled factional behaviour by these means, however, for though they could make it difficult for factions to fight and were able, eventually, to force it to the city margins, it proved resilient. Had the adherents of faction been allowed freer rein, it is likely that that the diverse factional interests established in Dublin city and environs in the course of the 18th century would have fought on a more regular basis, but the authorities were able to deploy enough resources to ensure that they were confined temporally as well as geographically. None the less, the identification of the Ormond and Liberty Boys with urban faction, reflected in the title of this work, is justified not only because they are correctly seen as its most striking manifestations, but also because they were the most enduring representatives of a social phenomenon that was as emblematic of 18th-century Dublin as other more socially agreeable, and better known, practices. Factional activity was not a constant in Dublin during the 18th century or even during the four decades spanning the late-1720s to the late-1760s that its major organizational manifestations – the Kevan Bail, the Ormond and the Liberty Boys – operated. Rather, this activity peaked in short-lived episodes – 1729–32, 1734–7, 1739–42, 1748, 1750–1, 1765–9 – separated by longer periods when faction went underground or assumed other forms. This study seeks to explore why this was so, and to progress understanding of one of the defining features of certain local communities in eighteenth-century Ireland.

The implication, that community identity sometimes formed around forces that were socially disruptive, and that were inherently disharmonious is not novel, but it does not accord with the intrinsically benign view of community, 'based on harmony of belief and opinion', articulated by H.P.R. Finberg and identified with the Leicester school of local historians.[15] What the pattern of factional behaviour practiced by rival communities in 18th-century Dublin suggests is that once the social, economic and demographic conditions necessary to sustain a local community were in place that identity could take different forms, and that in some instances internal coherence was generated by a readiness to engage in acts of aggression targeted at other communities who operated according to similar principles.

1. The Kevan Bail and the commencement of factional disorder

In common with their rural counterparts, urban factions required a strong sense of locational and group identity. Conditions conducive to their development in Dublin were not in place until the early 18th century, when, as a result of the phase of urban growth that had commenced in the 1660s, a series of new and greatly expanded suburban communities were developed. Fuelled by the rapid growth registered over the course of the first half of the 17th century that had seen the population increase more than fourfold – from an estimated 10,000 to 45,000 between 1600 and 1685 – the city continued to grow at an impressive rate. Disagreement over the size of households complicates the calculation of the pace of demographic expansion, but whether one employs Patrick Fagan's mean household size of 9.3 persons or David Dickson's more cautious figure (8 persons), the population of the city more than doubled between 1685 and 1730. The pace of growth may have moderated thereafter, as the effects of famine conditions in the late 1720s and early 1740s and a developing pattern of emigration took hold, but the city's population remained on a defiantly upwards trajectory, rising (according to Dickson) from an estimated 140,000 in 1760 to 154,000 in 1778. The fact that an expanding percentage of this growth was accounted for by a disproportionate rise in the Catholic component of the population, which increased from an estimated 33 to 39 per cent between 1715 and 1733, and attained numerical parity with the hitherto larger Protestant component by the early 1750s, is particularly noteworthy; it reinforced the tendency, already evident in the increased economic activity and new residency patterns permitted by the physical expansion of the city, for communities of people of the same religion, social status and employment to congregate in distinct areas of the city.[1]

This expansion was most noticeable on the north side of the river Liffey as a result, in the first instance, of the efforts of the Corporation to promote growth by making land available to individuals to develop. A major step was taken in 1665 with the development of an outline streetscape in the Smithfield area and the applotment of just short of 100 sites along the new or reconfigured thoroughfares of Channel Row, King Street, Queen Street and Smithfield (fig. 2). Consistent with the aspiration to establish 'a new high status suburb', land was also granted in the area to the duke of Ormond, and to the newly-founded King's Hospital, or 'Blue Coat', school. This seemed likely to be achieved when just short of half of the 92 plots let to individuals were taken by peers (3), baronets (3), major officeholders (1), gentlemen (19)

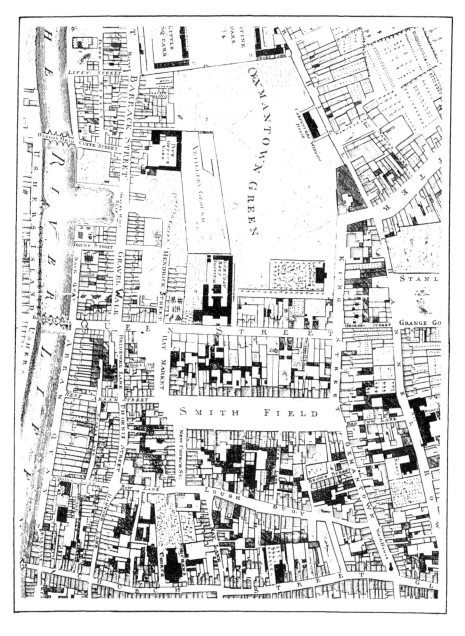

2 Map of Oxmantown and Smithfield, by John Rocque, 1756

and aldermen (17). A further 15 were taken by merchants but, in what was
to become an important pointer to its demographic future, the single largest
category were tradesmen, who accounted for more than one-third of the
total.[2] The significance of this was not apparent for some time, as an
encouraging number of lawyers, judges, officeholders and landowners chose
to reside in Smithfield and in nearby Oxmantown. They were encouraged
doubtlessly by the development in the area by Richard Tighe, who was
allocated a plot on Queen Street in 1665, of a Bowling Green, and by the
undertaking by William Ellis, in return for a favourable lease of the river
frontage between Queen Street and the Phoenix Park, to construct 'a quay
along the river to the Parke gate'.[3] However, by the early 18th century, the
proximity of the Royal Barracks (1706) and commercial centres such as the
butter market on Oxmantown Green, combined with more socially attractive
developments on the south side of the river, particularly along St Stephen's
Green and Dawson Street, which were not similarly encumbered, diminished its appeal to the elite, and it steadily acquired a more commercial, and
less exclusive, profile.[4]

Meanwhile to the east of Smithfield, Humphrey Jervis's willingness to
answer the call of the earl of Essex and oversee the construction at
considerable personal cost of a new bridge (Essex Bridge) across the Liffey
in the late 1670s paved the way for the development of lands near the river
that were previously largely 'waste'. Jervis revealed his ambitious vision for
the area by laying it out in streets 'in order to be built', and by spending
'several thousand pounds' walling the river and building Ormond Quay. He
also demonstrated that he was a formidable political operator by availing of
his nomination to successive terms as lord mayor in the early 1680s to
convince the corporation to implement the instruction of the privy council
of 2 March 1683 and move the main public markets (grain and live cattle
excepted) from their cramped and inconvenient locations at Fishamble
Street, Crane Lane, St John's Lane and elsewhere in 'the old city to his new
grounds'.[5] Located on a large site off the quay between Essex Bridge and
Ormond Bridge, and named Ormond market in honour of the then lord
lieutenant, the duke of Ormond, the relocation across the river of the stalls
of the butchers, bakers, fishmongers, sellers of herbs, roots, vegetables,
potatoes and fruit, butter, cheese and other commodities was not easily
achieved. However, Jervis' persistence paid off, and he deserves primary
credit for the transformation of the area from the fieldscape depicted in
Bernard de Gomme's 1673 map into the teeming commercial quarter with
its dense network of new streets recorded by Charles Brooking in 1728.[6]
Significantly, and in keeping with the opportunities presented by the
presence of the main city market, the social profile of the area was
emphatically 'lower class'. It was also predominantly Catholic, which set it
apart from the wealthier residential developments promoted by the

3 Map of Ormond Market and Ormond Quay, by John Rocque, 1756

Drogheda, Dominick and Gardiner interests to the north and east of Jervis's sphere of activity in the course of the eighteenth century (fig. 3).[7]

The impressive network of residential, commercial and recreational developments that were put in place on the northern side of the Liffey from the 1660s could not have occurred without the extension of the walling of the river. Furthermore, their creation obliged municipal officials to recognise that, because 'the city of late is much enlarged [and] grown more populous', it required 'more attendance in the chief magistrates government thereof'.[8] An important administrative innovation, approved in 1697, was the division of St Michan's parish, which embraced the whole of the north side, and which accounted for an estimated 22 per cent of the adult population of the city at the end of the seventeenth century, into three new parishes – St Paul's to the west embraced Smithfield and Oxmantown; St Michan's in the centre encompassed Ormond market, and St Mary's, which was the more easterly. It was an appropriate initiative as each grew rapidly in the early 18th century – by 81 per cent, 51.4 per cent and 235 per cent respectively between 1701 and 1718 – according to a contemporary survey of the number of houses in the capital.[9]

The pace of growth on the more developed southern side of the river as indicated by the same survey was less dramatic, though the number of houses rose in all parishes, and by over 50 per cent in those, namely St Andrew's, St Katherine's and St Peter's, where the pressure to build was greatest and land for construction was readily available.[10] This resulted in the emergence of wealthy new areas, particularly on the eastern margins of the city around St Stephen's Green and environs (St Peter's and St Anne's parishes), but it also facilitated the expansion and consolidation of existing communities, with distinctly lower social profiles, around the Coombe and Thomas Street, and the emergence of sizeable new communities defined by occupation as well as by geography in the Liberties to the west of Meath Street, along the Upper Coombe, New Street and, later, off Cork Street and Weavers' Square (fig. 4).

It took time for these communities to reach a size sufficient to sustain a local identity, but it was facilitated in the enclave of St Kevan's port by the fact that it was located in the archbishop's liberty, which was outside the city boundary. Separated from the rest of Dublin by its location and by its history, its distinctiveness was accentuated by its difficult relationship with Dublin corporation, which aspired to embrace it within its jurisdiction. This was already an issue in 1687 when the clerk of the Court of King's Bench petitioned the corporation for the payment of fees due arising out of 'severall traversed records and presentments' he had prepared 'concerneing St Kevans Port'.[11] Twelve years later, in 1699, the corporation further demonstrated its unwillingness to accede to St Kevan's Port separateness when the lord mayor and sheriffs were instructed 'to goe to St Kevans Port, and there assert the cities right to the customes of the said port' and 'the citty agent' was authorised to contest 'any suite or trouble attending their so doeing'.[12] Disputes of this kind were frequently prolonged, not least because the case in favour of imposing a uniform system of administration, such as the corporation sought in this instance, clashed with the traditional entitlement of St Patrick's Liberty to determine its own affairs, and it is noteworthy that the Liberty sustained its right to convene a court leet into the 1770s.[13]

The sense of local identification this encouraged was reinforced by an expanding range of communal celebrations and protests. The importance of the annual commemorations held on 1 July, 4 November and other dates in affirming Protestant identity is well established.[14] Less is known of the impact of more localised events on local populations like that of St Patrick's Liberty, which revelled in honouring Jonathan Swift, the dean of St Patrick's Cathedral, at every opportunity. Some of these occasions, such as the birthday gathering in 1726 when 'several societies of worthy gentlemen' processed 'with great solemnity and rejoicings' to the cathedral for prayers and subsequently to Vicar's Hall in St Patrick's Close for a musical entertainment, may seem rather exclusive, but the accompaniment of bell ringing and bonfires had a tangibly wider local appeal, and it is not without significance that these became central features of such events.[15] Swift certainly served as a focus of identity in this area of Dublin, as was manifested in January 1734 when a rumour that 'a certain person had openly threatened … to stab or maim him' prompted 'the inhabitants of the Liberty' to process to the deanery with an offer to protection.[16] Encouraged by such displays, the population of the area were prepared to make their sentiments known on other issues, as they demonstrated in April 1733 when they gathered before bonfires at the Steeple in St Patrick's Liberty and at the dean's house to celebrate the defeat of a controversial excise bill at Westminster.[17]

The fact that this protest was prompted in the first instance by the apprehension that the ratification of the excise bill must lead to higher prices indicates that faction flourished in an economic environment in which few enjoyed a comfortable living or possessed deep reserves. This was highlighted by the minister and churchwardens of the parish of St Werburgh's, when they observed of the area in 1715 that, apart from Dublin Castle, the Custom House and its attendant wealthy commercial heartland, the parish was 'inhabited chiefly by shopkeepers and tradesmen', whose capacity to contribute in any meaningful way to parish initiatives like church refurbishment was strictly limited.[18] The petitioners accounted for this by reference to the high rents demanded on properties in Dublin at the time, when they might with equal justification have cited the testing challenges experienced by tradesmen in the fast changing economic milieu of the early 18th century.

The main organisational casualties of the less regulated economic environment that came into being were the guilds, which were no longer able to assure craftsmen, who acceded to their strict personal as well as economic disciplines, that they would progress over time through the ranks to master craftsman, because the economic climate could no longer accommodate so many of the latter. The impact of this on the traditional pattern of employment was profoundly disruptive, for though many traditional practices endured and the guilds themselves remained influential in most trades, they were greatly diminished in their capacity to control apprentices and journeymen. This was vividly revealed in Dublin in 1725 when the master worsted and silk weavers publicly protested at the practice of their 'apprentices absenting themselves from our service before they have duly served their lawful time of seven years'.[19] The response of journeymen was still more critical as, contrary to the expectation widely shared within the ruling elite that employees should passively accept their working conditions no matter how demanding,[20] journeymen increasingly assumed responsibility for representing their own grievances. This was evident in 1711 when weavers protested against the sale and wearing of imported calicos, but it acquired a more structured form in the shape of journeymen societies.[21] Though inherently conservative in that they were, as Toby Barnard has pointed out, 'modelled' on the corporations of their masters,[22] the existence of 19 such societies by the mid-1720s is a telling measure of the increased restlessness of the large, and expanding, constituency of young men released from the discipline that guild membership historically enjoined.[23] Because the instincts, as well as the interests, of many journeymen demanded that they were seen to behave responsibly, much of the energies of the larger and more developed societies was channelled during the 1720s and 1730s into conventional activities such as the annual procession, religious service and evening entertainment organised on their patron saint's day by the broadcloth weavers, journeymen tailors, shoemakers and butchers.[24] Such occasions performed a crucial bonding function in respect of these crafts, but these events were of wider social significance in that they also reinforced the identification of trades with different areas that helped ultimately to sustain factional activity. This is most readily identifiable in the journeymen tailors' practice of holding their religious services in parish churches on the southern side of the city, while the journeymen butchers preferred to congregate at St Michan's on the north side, not far from Ormond Market, which was their employment heartland.[25]

Annual gatherings such as these proved of particular value to journeymen when they joined in the form of associative behaviour – the combination – for which they are best known. Significantly, the testing economic environment of the late 1720s was a crucial moment in the development of combinations in Ireland as several journeymen societies – notably those of the tailors, linen weavers and smiths – formed combinations in pursuit of their demands for shorter hours and better pay.[26] While attempts by journeymen to secure improved conditions by withdrawing labour were greeted with predictable hostility by the authorities, the fact that journeymen societies indulged and that combinations encouraged riotous behaviour strengthened this conviction.[27] In 1731, for example, 'a great company of resolute young fellows', almost certainly weavers and their supporters, marched through Dublin 'with musick before them, declaring openly against fustian and callicoes, and tearing them off the wearers wherever they found them'.[28] This tendency towards riotousness was reinforced by the fact that relations between the journeymen of different crafts were not always harmonious. Specific incidents are not always readily identifiable, but a 'desperate skirmish' in Cork in 1729 between weavers and butchers resulted in a 'the crippling of many, and the loss of several lives by mortal wounds and bruises',[29] while in Dublin in 1724, the broad and narrow weavers publicly acknowledged the 'differences' that had divided them from the butchers when they promoted a united front in opposition to the attempt to impose copper coin (Wood's halfpence) on Ireland.[30]

The image this generates of a society in which new associative forms were taking shape, and where the forces of demographic expansion, rapid physical growth and structural commercial adjustment permitted where they did not promote the emergence of factional interests whose primary form of expression was violence becomes still clearer when the pattern of contemporary riotousness and disorder is assessed. Early 18th-century riots took different forms, but still more significant than their range and variety was the readiness of distinct interests to have recourse to violence as a form of social expression. It cannot be shown that this was a logical consequence of a relaxed attitude to life or a diminished apprehension of death that may have obtained, though the pattern of popular attendance at executions and the strong appetite for 'gallows speeches' indicate that death was firmly integrated within quotidian social routines.[31] More pertinently, the fact that so much of the violence of a factional character took place on rest days, Sundays most notably, when 'companys' of young men met to 'divert themselves with hurling, playing cat, jumping, etc',[32] or on occasions of communal festivity such as fairs, particularly those held during the late summer, is critical because it links the ritual of factional violence to a pattern of recreational activity that permitted such forms of social expression precisely because they were of a ritualised and, by definition, of a limited nature. Significantly, recorded instances of such behaviour in the environs of Dublin during the first three decades of the 18th century are not commonplace, but the correlation that can be drawn between fairs, notably those held annually at Donnybrook and near Oxmantown Green (St Bartholomew's fair) each August, and rioting is suggestive. Reports of a riot at Donnybrook in 1716 in which a man died; of a great quarrel in 1727 in which two men may have been killed and between 40 and 90 wounded; and of a fatal assault at St Bartholomew's fair in 1728 are certainly consistent with an emerging culture of factional violence.[33]

This culture also drew on a pattern of riotousness that was more obviously politically inspired, and on social tensions that prompted an increased number of violent incidents during the 1710s and 1720s. To date, most scholarly attention has focussed on the disturbances provoked by Jacobite students and the 'Catholic mob'.[34] The 'scandalous riots' fomented in 1715 by Trinity students on the duke of Ormond's birthday certainly animated Archbishop William King of Dublin's ire,[35] but these were essentially modest protests compared with those prompted by the 'Catholic mob', which assembled wearing white roses – the Jacobite symbol – at St Stephen's Green on 10 June during the 1720s to honour the Pretender's birthday. Much has been written about these events, but one of their striking features is how easily these ostensibly celebratory occasions escalated into riot. In June 1724, for example, the spark was provided by the appearance of a Quaker wearing a red rose; this prompted a 'skirmish' between some Jacobites and 'loyalists' in which 'several broken heads were … received and given on both sides' and the Jacobite crowd prevailed.[36] Two years later, on 10 June 1726, the 'great mob' that assembled at St Stephen's Green fared worse as the deployment of an army detachment to quell disturbances prompted initially by the throwing of dead cats at Lord Abercorn's house, in response to his objecting to the gathering, resulted in several protestors being 'desperately wounded', and between 30 and 60 being taken into custody.[37] This compelled the authorities to take decisive action, and the lord mayor's decision to ban assemblies of people wearing white roses ensured there was no repeat of such scenes in 1727.[38]

While this intervention served successfully to interrupt the developing pattern of riotous disorder on the Pretender's birthday, it did nothing to ease the already difficult relationship of the city's population with the military garrison, which is more revealing than the activities of the 'Catholic mob' of the population's riotous disposition. This was highlighted in August 1724 when the large 'concourse of people' that gathered at Oxmantown Green for the St Bartholomew's Day fair responded to the offensive behaviour of some soldiers from the Royal Barracks by attacking them with stones and staves, mortally wounding four. Six months later, another encounter at the same location between the 'mob' and the 'military' resulted in a substantial number of casualties on both sides, whilst across the river at the Cornmarket a bystander was killed when the local mob clashed with the Cameronian regiment in September 1724.[39] Further evidence of the growing disposition to riot, and of the greater participation by definable social groups is provided by the 'conflict' precipitated by the students of Trinity College in 1722 when they took such exception to the interruption of their view of the funeral of Lady Coghill, they provoked a fight with a body of citizenry that precipitated several deaths and many injuries, and by the readiness of 'two companys of strolling vagrants call'd *Mummers*' to inflict serious injury on each other on 26 December 1728.[40] Compared with these events, the disturbances prompted

4 Map of Kevan's Port, Long Lane and environs, by John Rocque, 1756

by political differences such as the bitter contest between whigs and tories over the Dublin mayoralty in the early 1710s and by opposition in 1724 to Wood's halfpence were bloodless affairs. So too were the food riots, sparked off by near famine conditions in Dublin in the spring of 1729, but their occurrence offers further evidence, as E.P. Thompson famously observed, of the popular legitimacy of limited purposeful rioting.[41]

II

In view of the varied manifestations of riotousness that can be identified, and the formative impact major demographic, social and economic forces had on the forging of local and sectoral identities in Dublin by the 1720s, the emergence of urban factions was a logical if not inevitable development. The first to achieve notoriety was the Kevan Bail (alternatively known as the Keven or Cavan Bail), which acquired its emblematic name by combining that of the locality out of which it emerged (St Kevan's Port and its environs in the liberty of St Patrick's: see fig. 4) with the activity – the 'frequent rescue of prisoners out of the hands of police officers' – which made them notorious. Though their stern Protestantism has tempted some to portray the Kevan Bail in primarily sectarian terms, and to suggest that their priority from the start was with 'battling' their better-known Catholic equivalent, the Ormond Boys, this cannot be sustained since the latter hardly existed in an organised form when the 'Butchers of St Patrick's', which was how the Bail were then misleadingly described, initially made their presence felt. Moreover, their first recorded encounters dating from April 1729 were not with the Catholic 'mob' but with the weavers of the Coombe, as a result of which a 'young' nailer, John Handlon, was killed.[42] Clashes of this seriousness and scale inevitably attracted the notice of the authorities, who, as well as intervening to prevent riots in progress, sought to pre-empt their recurrence by detaining those responsible. This set the butchers at loggerheads with the city constables and prompted the rescues, whereby the 'Butchers of St Patrick' became the Kevan Bail.[43] It was an appropriate redesignation since one of their first responses to the attempt to curb their activities was to exclude outsiders 'that [*sic*] pretends to come from the city into their *precincts*'.[44] Significantly, the Bail were less respectful of the territories of others; as well as their practice of assembling nightly in the Kevan's Port area, they engaged in riotous encounters at St Stephen's Green, the court house and the Strand. They also joined briefly in a tactical alliance with the Smithfield mob, who acquired the name the Smithfield Bail at this time, in targeting John Hawkins and other constables, climaxing in 'a desperate skirmish with many constables' early in June.[45] This was an indicative action, since it suggests that factional interests prioritised the defence of their right to settle quarrels without reference to those officially charged with the maintenance of law and order. This was not something the authorities could countenance, though it took the 'outrage' the Kevan Bail perpetrated on 10 June 1729 when they 'marched from St Kevin's Liberty to the city' to take on a 'large crowd wearing white roses', and the riots during the following nights to galvanize officialdom into decisive action.[46]

In a determined attempt to put a halt to the increasing daring of the Bail, the lords justice and privy council approved a proclamation on 21 June bearing the names of 30 men with the promise of a reward of £10 for each of the first ten apprehended and £5 for the remainder.[47] The men in question were described as butchers and yeomen 'of the Poddle', and the fact that one of those styled a 'yeoman' was denominated a 'cobbler' elsewhere implies that the majority were tradesmen. This is certainly consistent with the pattern of employment in the area. The fact that one of those named – Edmond Knight, alias Blacknight – bore the same *soubriquet* as a man tried for involvement in a weavers' combination in 1731 may give further authority to this conclusion.[48] No women were among those proclaimed in June, or included on the supplement produced by the lord mayor in February 1730, but the detention of five women and three men at the house of a chimney sweep in Bull Alley in August 1729 on the grounds that they were member of the Bail intimates that participation was not gender exclusive, though there is little or no evidence to indicate that women took an active part in hostilities.[49]

Fighting was not the priority of the Kevan Bail in the late summer of 1729, for though they contrived in the aftermath of the appearance of the privy council proclamation and another by Dublin corporation in July to sustain their struggle with the constables of the city for a time, and to fight with, and to punish impostors at Donnybrook fair in August, the number of incidents attributable to the Bail soon fell away sharply.[50] There were atrocities, such as the attack by 'five or six' bailsmen on 18 August in which Thomas Gillmor, a trooper in one of the horse regiments, was 'barbarously wounded' and one of his assailants mortally hurt, but such increasingly were the work of gangs comprised of three to six members, and were more redolent of crime than factional activity.[51]

The success of the authorities' strategy to disrupt the Bail by targeting known activists was the primary reason for this shift in emphasis. The authorities certainly underlined their commitment to deter factional disorder when the privy council's decision in August to renew its previous proclamation offering rewards for 30 named men for riot, was echoed by Dublin corporation in September, and by a number of newspapers, which republished the list of identified offenders.[52] A number had already been detained, but the success of the authorities in apprehending known Bailsmen and their accomplices, female as well as male, increased appreciably in the autumn and winter of 1729–30.[53] By February 1730, 15 of the 30 men proclaimed the previous June had been taken into custody, and while the number of known activists at large was still sizeable at 21, as a result of the identification of a further six individuals, it was an encouraging result.[54] The authorities were assisted in achieving this by both the fear of detection and by the offer of an indemnity to those of the Bail that turned approver. Another important factor was the eagerness of some to reach an accommodation with the authorities, which prompted a number of those who were proclaimed to seek immunity from prosecution by betraying colleagues. The most notable such incident occurred in July when James Wheeler, Michael Jones and Hugh Reily bundled Edmond 'Blacknight' Knight into a coach destined for the city's main prison, Newgate; Knight incurred severe injuries in the process, but successfully overpowered his captors and escaped.[55]

Though this attempt to apprehend one of its leading members proved unsuccessful, the capacity of the authorities to curb the Kevan's Bail was enhanced by the impact of their efforts to improve discipline among the constables that comprised the Dublin watch. This involved dismissing those whose 'honesty' could not be assumed, prosecuting others who were suspected of criminal behaviour, and establishing a tighter command and deployment structure.[56] No less indicatively, it was determined to improve the effectiveness of the courts by decreeing that the main city court, the Court of Oyer and Terminer, should meet monthly, like the Old Bailey in London.[57] Since this pattern of sitting was not inaugurated until March 1732, it had no obvious impact on the decline in the activities of the Kevan Bail in 1730 and 1731. Rather, credit for this rests with the ongoing policy of arrest and prosecution of those suspected of involvement, which resulted in the capture of further activists, two of who were executed in March 1730.[58] This sent a strong message to the remainder, but much more damaging in the long run to the capacity of the Bail to operate was the authorities' decision in December 1730 to order 30 of their number, who were unable 'to provide sufficient security for their good behaviour' if they were released from confinement, to transportation to North Carolina; it inflicted a permanent blow from which the Bail never really managed to recover.[59] The fact that other members of the Bail chose to take their leave of the city, and still more to embrace criminality were further debilitating influences.[60]

2. The Ormond and Liberty Boys, 1730–70

Though the combination of legal prosecution, culminating in the decision in 1730 to transport a substantial number of activists, and the disengagement of many others for fear of the consequences ensured the Kevan Bail did not begin the 1730s in a strong position, it did not just fade from view. Reports in the spring and summer of 1732 of 'riots' and 'quarrels' in the Kevin's Port area involving the Bail, the army and diverse groups, of whom the weavers from the earl of Meath's Liberty were the most notable, attested to its resilience.[1] More importantly, the impulse that sustained faction grew stronger in the early 1730s, for while the Kevan Bail endeavoured to regroup, the weavers of Liberties and the butchers of Ormond Market, which was now firmly established as 'the principal market' in the city, and Smithfield came gradually to assume a higher profile.[2] Neither body answered at this point to the appellations (the Liberty and Ormond Boys) by which they were to achieve notoriety, but the gradual escalation of their conflicts facilitated the formation of a distinctive factional identity in each case that was well established before the end of the decade.

Deriving as much from a long-standing tradition of suspicion as from the identifiably new factional impulse represented by the Kevan Bail, the signal for the inauguration of a more violent relationship between the weavers of the Liberties and the butchers of the south river parishes was provided, beginning late in 1729, by the action of a body of weavers, who took cattle from Smithfield market for the popular recreational practice of baiting them with dogs. Since bull baiting was a 'sport' in which the butchers adopted a proprietorial attitude, the weavers' intrusion into Smithfield, which was butchers' territory, was deemed doubly insulting and the butchers felt honour bound to respond. The violence that ensued did not conform to any obvious pattern at first, but because competitive violence of this kind tended to be self-perpetuating, the two factions met with increasing frequency till by the spring of 1731 they were meeting 'almost every Sabath'.[3] The injuries inflicted on those occasions were consistent with the employment of 'stones and clubs', which were the weapons of choice of factions at this time.[4] However, the preparedness of butchers to employ the tools of their trade, and, follow-ing the example of some street robbers, to use them on occasion to inflict serious injuries, including the butcher's signature punishment of houghing or hamstringing their victims, was an ominous pointer to the greater violence of their clashes in the future.[5] This seldom happened in the early 1730s because factions were largely content to engage in what one commentator termed 'a smart skirmish' in which bruises and breaks rather than lost limbs and life threatening injuries were the norm.[6]

This pattern of limited violence served to encourage rather than to discourage factionalism. The most striking indicator of this is provided by the fact that, in addition to the encounters involving the Oxmantown and Coombe 'mobs', as the Ormond butchers and Liberties weavers were commonly labelled in the early 1730s, the roster of factional bodies was augmented by the emergence of the Stoneybatter mob and by groups of tradesmen such as the shoemakers, who engaged variously with each other, and with the watch and the military at a variety of public locations of which Oxmantown Green, Smithfield and Kilmainham Common were the most popular.[7] Fairs were another option, but though they continued to produce more than their share of fatal assaults, the presence of constables made these less inviting venues than open greens and commons.[8] The latter locations may also have appealed because they permitted the pre-fight challenges and coat-trailing that were integral to faction fighting in the countryside during the 19th century, though it cannot be shown that they took the same form in 18th-century Dublin. It certainly required planning and direction to bring a faction into action, and it can be assumed that these were among the responsibilities of faction leaders. This is not to suggest that such factional encounters as took place in the early 1730s were contrived; fighting was integral to factionalism, and it was thus logical as well as necessary for them to demonstrate their fighting prowess through engagement. This was made all the more likely in the case of the Ormond butchers and the Liberty weavers by their proximity, and by the fact that they were fast emerging as the largest and most active factions in the city. The enmity this generated may have been accentuated, as has been suggested, by atavistic confessional suspicions (the Liberties in which the weavers were based was predominantly Protestant, while a census taken of St Michan's parish in 1723 established that as much as two-thirds of its population was Catholic).[9] However, if this is so, it was not visible at the time, and it was subordinate to the factional commitment borne out of local and group identification.

Some insight into the strength of the still emerging commitment to faction can be provided by citing the readiness of definable commercial and social interests such as the smiths, who engaged with the porters in Crane Lane in April 1731, the chairmen who clashed with 'the Gentlemen's servants' in February 1732, and the students of Trinity College, who sustained a dispute with the city mob and the watch throughout the early 1730s, to conduct themselves in a manner redolent of faction.[10] But a more telling perspective is offered by the treatment meted out to Paul, alias 'Gallows Paul', Farrell in 1734. As one of the constables, who had engaged actively in the pursuit of the Kevan Bail (he was publicly applauded for taking Michael Kelso, one of the proclaimed Bail in July 1730) and in apprehending 'riotous weavers' in

1733, Farrell was a hate figure with faction and journeymen interests across the city. The contempt in which he was held was intensified by his unsavoury personal reputation, which ensured that few expressed any sympathy when he was 'seized' by the Ormond Boys whilst *en route* with a prisoner to Kilmainham jail in August 1734. It would not have been unexpected, given the threats levelled in 1729 by the Kevan Bail that they would whip any constable that fell into their hands, if Farrell should suffer the same fate. However, rather than reserve the pleasure of punishing him to themselves, the Ormond Boys demonstrated an unexpected degree of solidarity with their main factional rivals by contacting the Liberty Boys and inviting them to join with them in devising a suitable sanction for Farrell. What followed bore closer comparison to a lynching than a judicial hearing because of the brutal way in which Farrell forfeited his life, but the fact that the two groups joined together in its administration offers a vivid illustration of the strength of factional commitment as well as of the capacity of those who embraced it to engage in acts of extreme violence.[11]

Though no reference was made to economic conditions in the extensive reporting of the episode, the fact that Farrell was hung on a tree in Weaver's Square and that the textile sector of the economy was operating in a particularly difficult trading environment in the early 1730s suggests that the pent-up anger to which Farrell fell victim was more than just personalised animus. The journeymen weavers certainly seemed to have a strong case for higher wages since, as they pointed out, 'their wages are not half as much as an English day-labourer'. Unwilling to accede to this intolerable state of affairs, the weavers of the Coombe and other textile operatives contrived to improve their circumstances by enforcing a variety of restrictive practices aimed at maintaining wage levels. They engaged in combinations; they promoted the consumption of home manufacture, and, when these measures did not have the desired effect, they supported attacks in 1734 on the shops of woollen drapers that stocked textiles of English manufacture, and in 1735 on persons wearing garments of foreign origin.[12] Though essentially economically inspired and thus ostensibly remote from the world of factional violence, the anger and despair that fuelled such actions also nourished the emotions that drove faction. There are many telling incidents, but the most revealing are the encounters involving journeymen, such as occurred early in July 1732, when the journeymen tailors and shoemakers fought on consecutive nights in St John's Lane and Winetavern Street, and in May 1733, when 'there was a great battle between the people of the … Earl of Meath's Liberty … and those of … the Archbishop of Dublin's, wherein several were wounded on each side'.[13]

Acutely conscious of the implications both for the peace of the city and for the preservation of harmony among the predominantly Protestant artisan class that lived in the industrial parishes to the south of the river, local interests headed by the marshals of the Liberty of St Sepulchre and of the Liberty of Thomas Court and Donore brokered a truce whereby the journeymen of both jurisdictions pledged 'a cessation of arms' for twelve months.[14] This proved more stable than might have been anticipated, and it served successfully to bring the inter- and intra-factional violence in these Liberties to an end. However, it did not diminish the factional impulse that was firmly established in this area of the city. On the contrary, it may have contributed, along with the sense of communal beleaguerment attributable to the difficult commercial environment, to the elision of the differences and divisions that had separated many south side factions. This was crucial to the emergence of the Liberty Boys as, not just the dominant, but the representative Liberty faction. Significantly, a similar process seems to have been taking place on the north side of the city, where it is still more difficult to trace. It does appear, however, that the emergence of the Ormond Boys as the major north-side faction was made possible by the coming together of the butchers, a popular contemporary designation which, as well as skilled operatives, embraced 'assistants and carriers from slaughter-houses', of Ormond Market, the 'cattle drivers' of Smithfield and the 'stable boys, helpers and porters' of Ormond Quay.[15] This formative development may have taken place in both locations somewhere between the conclusion of the Liberties 'truce' in May 1733 and the murder of Paul Farrell in August 1734, since the first identifiable usage of the appellations 'Ormond Boys' and 'Liberty Boys' was in the reports detailing the involvement of both factions in the apprehension and mistreatment of Farrell.[16] Then, the novelty of the term was signalled by the continuing employment of the cumbersome original – 'the boys of Ormond market and those of the Liberty'.[17] Within a few years, the more felicitous terms by which these factions are best known had achieved common currency and before long, news reports observed that both factions 'called themselves' by these names.[18] By then too, the public had adjusted to the fact that the competitive character of factions was such that these, the most distinct and powerful factions in the city, were locked in an intense rivalry that effectively ensured that the main frontier of factional activity was north-south across the river Liffey.

This was manifest in February 1734 when 'several of the inhabitants of the Liberty got together in a tumultuous manner and fought against the butchers of Ormond and Castle market'.[19] The prompt intervention of the constables prevented this escalating into something more serious, and the vigilance of the authorities proved no less crucial on a number of other occasions during the same year when there were threatened surges in faction-authored violence. One such instance occurred in October when the weavers' engagement in baiting a bull they had taken from Smithfield was interrupted by the lord mayor; on another occasion, an attack by some drunken members of the Kevan Bail on a body of carmen was disrupted.[20]

This inaugurated a trend that was to continue as the combination of official alertness, and the disinclination of the main factions to test the authorities' resolve ensured the initiative remained with the former during the mid-1730s. This was highlighted by the public whipping of those taken up for rioting, and by the prosecution of a number of 'Liberty Boys' and others for murder when fatalities ensued from riotous conduct, which were the most visible manifestations of a security policy aimed at disrupting faction at source.[21] The importance, and effectiveness, of this approach was demonstrated in 1735 when indications that the Kevan Bail was beginning to stir once more prompted the doubling of the city guard and the placement of a detachment at the lower end of Kevin's Street, as a result of which a number of known 'rioters' were apprehended and imprisoned for a year, others were subject to the indignity of a public whipping, and 'seven of the ringleaders … were all order'd for transportation'.[22] A less high profile version of the same policy pursued in 1736 proved equally effective in curbing riotousness from the same quarter,[23] while the efforts of Dublin corporation in the late 1730s to minimise the opportunity for riot by prohibiting the wearing of white roses in honour of the Pretender, by proscribing the erection of May bushes, by forbidding the setting up of booths at St James' fair, and by attempting to proscribe bull baiting, on the grounds that all were 'pernicious to the peace and welfare' of the city, represented a further earnest of the resolve of the authorities to interdict all forms of riotous disorder.[24]

The effectiveness of the authorities' strategy to impede factional rioting during the mid-1730s is best demonstrated by the fact that such encounters as took place during these years involved lesser known and generally short-lived factions like the 'mob of St James's Street', which engaged in 'a very great fray' on Twatling Street with a 'great number of soldiers' and apprentice skinners in June 1736 when 'several persons were desperately wounded and maimed'.[25] Rioting was also reported in the same year in the earl of Meath's Liberty on St John's eve, and in October when a body of Kevan Bail clashed with and was put to flight by the residents of Big Ship Street.[26] The problems the authorities faced, and to which they had no answer, was that the efforts they made to promote social order and to regulate public behaviour at fairs did little to dilute the commitment of the residents of St Patrick's Liberty, the earl of Meath's Liberty, Ormond Market and elsewhere to their local faction, as evidenced by their continuing readiness 'to meet, and try, what they falsely call each other's manhood' by physical force.[27]

In these circumstances, it was to be anticipated when a new, intensified phase to faction-inspired disorder followed the improvement in economic fortunes from 1736 that the Ormond and Liberty Boys would feature as the most persistent combatants. This was not apparent initially as the Kevan Bail maintained its traditionally high visibility, but by the end of 1736 it was no longer a faction of consequence and, from this point onwards, the struggle for pre-eminence between the Liberty and Ormond Boys was the dominant rivalry in the sphere of Dublin faction.[28] This was particularly noticeable during the fair season (which spanned the late summer – early autumn months) of 1737 when, rather than continue their preferred practice and meet at Kilmainham Common, the two clashed at St James's fair in late July, at Palmerstown fair in early August and at Donnybrook Fair in mid-August.[29] Moreover, having encountered little opposition from the authorities, the factions brought the struggle to the city streets, with the result that before the end of August further 'battling and fighting' involving both sides was reported on the south side at Patrick Street and Plunket Street in the heart of the Liberties and at Castle Market off Dame Street and, on the north side close to the markets at Pill Lane and Smithfield.[30] Since stones and wooden clubs were the main weapons employed on these occasions, the number of fatalities that resulted was seldom large. Three people in all (two at St James, and one at Palmerstown) were killed at the fair meetings, but the violence was intensifying, as evidenced by the fact that serious injuries consistent with the employment of knives and bayonet became increasingly commonplace.[31]

Spurred into action once more by the visible deterioration in public order caused by the 'great numbers of idle and disorderly persons who have … riotously and unlawfully assembled themselves … in the streets', the lord mayor of Dublin James Somervell issued a proclamation on 19 August 1737, appealing to employers and householders to 'restrain their respective apprentices and servants from joining in any riot or unlawful assembly', and instructing 'all inhabitants' to retire to 'their own houses and places of abode' when riot threatened.[32] The privy council endorsed this strategy on 19 September by commanding the 'Lord Mayor … sheriffs, … justices of the peace and other magistrates and officers' to 'take the most effectual means for preventing and suppressing such riots and tumultuous assemblies'. Galvanized by this instruction, and by a vote of £50 approved by the Corporation to imburse those who inaugurated successful prosecutions, those entrusted with enforcing the law were enabled to regain the initiative.[33] As they had done previously with the Kevan Bail, they set about undermining the capacity of both the Ormond and Liberty Boys to sustain their factional activities by identifying and arresting their leaders. Their most notable target was Thady Foy, 'the captain or head of the Liberty Boys', who was tried and found guilty of murdering a watchman; he was subsequently hanged and quartered at the Tholsel on 12 November.[34] The sentences handed down in the case of the Ormond Boys, who were rounded up and charged with riot were less severe (several were sentenced to a public whipping), but it is significant that they too were subjected to exemplary punishments.[35]

Measured by the references to reported riots, which is the primary register of such activity, the authorities were successful in preventing a repetition in

1738, and in the years immediately following, of the rage of factional violence witnessed in 1737. This result was achieved at a considerable price, however, since in addition to banning St James's fair in 1738 and an attempt to eradicate bull baiting, it was recommended that aldermen should be empowered, when they possessed reliable evidence, to commit 'idle, disorderly persons, rioters or vagabonds' to Newgate prison.[36] This does not seem to have come to pass, but one of the consequences of the intensified security efforts to curb factional disorder was a visible deterioration in civil-military relations that had longer-term implications for the way in which the main factions conducted themselves. It is striking, moreover, that this was more marked in respect of the Ormond Boys. It was neither prompted nor animated by the 'great riot' that began at Oxmantown Green and continued on Dirty Lane and Thomas Street on Sunday, 23 April 1738 in which the army 'cut and most desperately wounded' a 'great number' of Ormond Boys, but such events certainly encouraged large swathes of an already suspicious public to conclude that they could not rely on the military for the impartial application of the law.[37] The consequences of this were revealed a month later when a number of butchers (Ormond Boys) set upon the St Michan's parish watch in Charles Street, killing one and severely wounding two others.[38] In order to make clear their revulsion and to discourage a repetition of this event, the authorities decreed that Bryan May, who was found guilty of the murder, should be executed on the quays close to the site of the crime. This punishment had the hoped for effect of helping to keep the city pacific in the second half of 1738, but its effect was temporary.[39] When rioting between the Ormond and Liberty Boys recommenced with 'a pitch'd battle' on Oxmantown Green in the spring of 1739, the Liberty Boys were supported by some of the soldiers garrisoned in the city, who shared their antipathy to the Ormond Boys. It did not save them from defeat, and the soldiers' breach of discipline was not overlooked by their superiors. Four soldiers were subject to the harsh sanction of military discipline 'for assisting the Liberty Boys against the Ormond', but despite this exemplary action, the connection endured, and soldiers participated on the side of the Liberty Boys in factional rioting a decade later.[40]

Guided by such indicative incidents as well as by the denominational demography of the Liberties and Ormond Market areas, the suggestion, advanced by Sean Murphy and endorsed by Vincent Morley, that there was now an obvious sectarian dimension to the factional rivalry that bound the Ormond and Liberty Boys seems justified.[41] This cannot be ruled out, as the report that Edward McDonogh, one of the leaders of the Ormond Boys, 'uttered treasonable words at the head of his party' in September 1748 intimates, but it is significant that he was about to lead his faction into battle with 'some soldiers' at Oxmantown Green, and that there is no suggestion that similar sentiments were expressed before meetings with the Liberty

Boys then or at any other time.[42] Moreover, it is apparent that the impulse
which prompted factions of the same confessional allegiance to engage on a
regular basis did not require such motivation to sustain it. The Ormond Boys
and Liberty Boys were destined to be at loggerheads simply because each
aspired to dominate the other, and inferences that they were prompted by
sectarian convictions based on the prevailing confessional profile of their place
of origin seem particularly suspect. This is not to suggest that the readiness
of 'the vast number of Protestants' resident in the Liberties, to 'form …
themselves into companies of militia' in 1739 in order to assist with the
defence of the kingdom 'in case of an attack' from Catholic Europe, was
without ideological import, and of no significance in persuading some
soldiers to assist the Liberty Boys.[43] It can likewise be maintained that the
invocation of 'treasonable words' by Edward MacDonogh, cited above, is
ideologically revealing of the prejudices and inclinations of the Ormond
Boys. However, in the absence of evidence demonstrating conclusively that
the rivalry that impelled the Ormond and Liberty Boys to fight each other
was overtly sectarian, it seems prudent to account for the readiness of a small
number of soldiers to join with the Liberty Boys by reference to their shared
loyalty to the crown as the fiftieth anniversary of the Battle of the Boyne
approached and the prospect of war loomed. It is noteworthy in this context
that when Kevin Street was bedecked with bunting honouring Admiral
Vernon's victory over the Spanish at Cartagena in 1741, the enthusiastic
celebration that ensued proceeded without reference to the religion of the
protagonists.[44] This was true also of the altercations involving the Ormond
and Liberty Boys; it is preferable for this reason to interpret their relationship
in primarily factional terms, since this was capable on its own of sustaining
their intense rivalry.

Saliently, despite the involvement of soldiers on the side of the Liberty
Boys, the level of factional activity during the late 1730s and early 1740s
remained below that which had prompted the authorities decisive intervention in the autumn of 1737. Identifiable instances of the resort to 'club
law' were not uncommon as the Ormond and Liberty Boys gathered
frequently for what the *Dublin Daily Post* described as 'the pleasure of
fighting'. In keeping with the relaxed attitude to violence implicit in this
observation, the number of fatalities that resulted remained modest though
serious injuries, consistent with the use of knives as well as cudgels, were
routine.[45] This was made more likely by the fact that the Ormond Boys,
emboldened by their ability in the late 1730s to secure their territory against
intrusion, pushed across river into the heartland of the Liberties with greater
frequency in 1740. There, as well as the expected encounters with the
Liberty Boys, they confronted the Paddy Boys of Francis Street, the boys of
Castle Market, whom they fought on Dame Street and Essex Street in
September, and the ubiquitous military.[46] Fatalities were no more likely on

these occasions than on those when they confined themselves to
Oxmantown Green, though this was not invariably the case, and it ensured
the authorities remained on the alert lest such incidents should escalate and
a new spiral of factional disorder result.[47] This remained the position during
the early and mid-1740s. Thus 'a great mob' heading in the direction of
Donnybrook fair was dispersed by the intervention of the high sheriff and a
party of soldiers in August 1741, but 'bloody battles' mostly fought at
irregular intervals on or near the quays or the Liffey bridges, in which
neither the Ormond nor Liberty Boys were able to inflict a decisive reversal
on the other, proved more difficult to interdict.[48]

If, as this suggests, an unstable equilibrium had been reached between the
authorities, who continued to issue proclamations and to offer rewards for
the apprehension of 'notorious rioters and other offenders', and the prac-
titioners of faction fighting, who continued on occasions 'to perform the
exercise of club law', the reality was that the authorities retained the upper
hand, as the main factions continued to meet infrequently during the mid-
1740s. This was demonstrated in 1748 when, in February, the under-sheriff
for Co. Dublin, James Crofton, dispersed a large crowd that had gathered at
Kilmainham Common to fight, and in August when he 'assist[ed] in pulling
down several tents that were erected there' as part of a community festival,
lest their presence should encourage the large crowd to stay on site and
fight. Crofton's intervention was decisive on both occasions, but the fact that
many of the estimated 2,000 present in February were 'armed with clubs,
hangers etc' illustrated as vividly as the continuing, if intermittently expressed,
disposition of the Ormond and Liberty Boys to quarrel that the culture that
esteemed factional activity and sanctioned the violent conflicts it sustained
remained vibrant. This was underlined during the late 1740s.[49]

II

There is no obvious reason why, after several years of low-level activity, factional violence should intensify once more in 1748. There was no apparent
diminution in the resolve or the capacity of the municipal authorities to
curb factional activity or, in so far as is observable, an increase in factional
commitment in the city. It is as if, having been prevented for so long from
establishing who was the stronger in the time honoured fashion of fighting,
the leaders of 'the two subsisting factions', which was how the *Dublin
Courant* tellingly described the Ormond and Liberty Boys in October 1750,
determined at some point early in 1748 to engage once more in a test of
strength.[50] This conclusion is given some authority by the contemporary
contention, expressed on a number of occasions in 1748, that the structures
of the factions were sufficiently developed to allow them to 'enter into an

immediate and lasting peace',[51] as well as by the fact that meetings 'to decide
the old quarrel' commenced at Oxmantown Green in January 1748, which
was not the usual time of the year. This unseasonable activity certainly
caught the authorities unawares, and encounters took place on 'several
Sundays' before the lord mayor, Robert Ross, was spurred into activity on
12 February.[52] Ross successfully dispersed the 'riotous multitude' that had
gathered at Oxmantown Green on this occasion, but the genie of faction
had escaped and it did not take long for rioting to spread to the city streets.
Every encounter was not reported but since, other than the 'riot' on Queen
Street in mid-April, in which Christopher Sheridan, a Newgate turnkey, was
killed, those that are recorded occurred on the south side of the river, it can
be suggested that the Ormond Boys were the aggressors as they engaged
with the Liberty Boys early in June at Kevan's Port, and on Aungier Street,
George's Lane and adjacent streets.[53]

The press accounts of these disturbances are predictably formulaic, but
the occurrence of factional violence so close to Dublin Castle was a source
of genuine concern for both the municipal and political authorities, and
their unease in this point was intensified by the ability of faction to 'rout' the
military detachments sent to curb them, as well as by the daily reports of the
life-threatening injuries inflicted. In an attempt to ensure that this should
not continue, the authorities imposed near curfew conditions on the public
to facilitate the military's response to the challenge to law and order. This
seemed to pay dividends, as the pressure thus brought to bear, combined
with strident condemnation 'from the altar of every Romish chapel in
Dublin', prompted the protagonists to conclude a 'cessation of arms' soon
afterwards.[54] In the event, it proved short-lived as, beginning at Palmerstown
early in August and Donnybrook later the same month, the opportunity of
the fair season was seized upon by the rival factions, and a succession of
fights ensued.[55] Significantly, they were more violent that those that had
previously taken place. It is impossible either to prove or to disprove the
claim made in *Faulkner's Dublin Journal* in October that over 300 Liberty and
Ormond Boys had 'lost their lives and limbs' over a two-year period prior to
that date, but it is not improbable given the intensity of the fighting that
took place in the autumn of 1748. The most telling incident, which took
place in the Phoenix park, arose out of an encounter at Palmerstown Fair on
10 August in the course of which Pat Connolly, one of the 'heroes' of the
Ormond faction, was captured by the Liberty Boys. Initially threatened with
death by hanging, he escaped this fate because the Liberty 'chief prevented'
it, though the latter's intervention did not save him from a severe beating
that almost achieved the same purpose. Connolly was 'hacked in so terrible a
manner' that, one report callously observed, he was past 'giving any farther
disturbance to the public'.[56] This raised the threshold of factional violence,
and within twenty-four hours the Ormond Boys demonstrated that they

were capable of doing likewise when they took one of their 'antagonists prisoner … and', the *Dublin Courant* reported, 'hamstring and used him in a barbarous manner'.[57] It was the prelude to a six-week period of intense rioting, whose most remarkable feature was an unprecedented sequence of encounters during the four Sundays of September, as the Ormond and Liberty Boys locked horns at every opportunity.[58]

Though the venues for these encounters – Oxmantown Green, James Street and Bloody Bridge – were at some remove from the political, administrative and commercial heartland of the city, the authorities were understandably unwilling to allow the Ormond and Liberty Boys to set the law at defiance. It was not just that fighting was seen as a manifestation of the lawlessness that respectable society was anxious to eradicate, the authorities were genuinely troubled by the attendant disruption and by the increasing number of serious injuries. This was due to the greater resort to swords (hangers and scimitars most usually), knives and firearms to supplement the customary reliance on stones, clubs and cudgels, but developments in this area were also a cause of concern. The traditional oaken club had given way to the falchion, which was made from the staves of oak casks that were hardened by smoking, sharpened on one side and bored at one end to provide a secure grip.[59] It was a deadly weapon, and while it was not mentioned by name by Lord Mayor Ross when he reiterated his earlier proclamation calling for public order on 1 October 1748, it was embraced within his generic reference to 'clubs, cuteaus and fire arms'. Significantly, he was joined on this occasion, in what looks like a co-ordinated effort to restore order, by the Roman Catholic Church, which, as well as reiterating extant 'prohibitions' barring rioters from receiving the Eucharist, warned Catholics on 2 October that 'joyning in riots' was both 'contrary to the laws of the land and the known principles of Christianity'.[60]

Though the frequent reiteration of appeals and admonitions of this kind may suggest they had little real impact, the fact they were accompanied in this instance by the targeted deployment of constables and watchmen at the Liffey bridges and other 'usual places of rioting' in an attempt to prevent factions meeting, and that the military guard was held at the ready broke the cycle of rioting, and law and order was restored before the end of October.[61] The lord mayor was widely praised for his part in bringing this about, but the reality, as on a number of previous occasions, was that the leaders of faction adjudged that it was tactically wise not to force the issue in the teeth of official and religious condemnation. The Ormond Boys went furthest in this respect. 'Eight of the most reputed leaders' of this faction publicly recanted of their involvement in St Mary's parish chapel, which was located at the junction of Jervis Street and Mary Street, on 16 October 'with all the appearance of submission and true repentance' in faces 'bathed in tears'.[62] As a result, there were few challenges to public order during the remainder of

1748 or 1749. This can be attributed in large part to the promptitude with
which the authorities responded to prevent 'riotous' gatherings of Liberty
and Ormond Boys in December 1748, March 1749, and at other times
escalating into major factional confrontations, as well as to the fact that some
at least of the more enthusiastic members of both factions were in custody.[63]
The fact that Dublin was gripped for most of 1749 by a divisive by-election
was also significant, since it seems to have absorbed the energies of many
Liberty Boys who might otherwise have been drawn into factional activity.[64]

The implication that the Liberty Boys campaigned in the 1749 Dublin
by-election is supported by the fact that once the poll was over, and Charles
Lucas, who was the hero of the politically marginalized, was in exile, the
previously quiescent Liberty and Ormond factions showed less inclination to
follow the instructions of their civil and religious leaders and 'behave …
with prudence and decency'.[65] A particular cause of concern for the
residents of the Liberties in the early 1750s was the poor market for their
fabrics, but their plight was not lost on the Ormond Boys as, following the
successful deployment of the military to frustrate the journeymen weavers'
efforts to inhibit the consumption of rival fabrics, the Liberty and Ormond
Boys joined forces against the army and watch.[66] This was an *ad hoc* arrange-
ment, forged for a particular purpose against a common enemy, and its
emergence did not prevent the usual clashes between both factions in April
and May.[67] Significantly, the prompt response of the civil authorities, who
offered rewards of £5 for each rioter taken and convicted, and of the Catholic
Church, which closed its chapels during the afternoon in anticipation that it
would encourage 'the common people' to remain at work and deprive them
of the 'excuse for going abroad', ensured there was no repetition in 1750 to
the level of disruption registered in 1748.[68] There was an identifiable increase in
factional activity on the commencement in August of the fair season, but
this was sustained with difficulty through the winter, as the energetic magistrate Isaac Drury and the lord mayor, Thomas Taylor, successfully ushered
many of the most hardened rioters into jail.[69] It was apparent also by this
date that some amongst both factions had had enough. This is most readily
attestable by the decision of the Liberty Boys to imitate the actions of the
leaders of the Ormond faction in October 1748 and renounce 'their former
unjustifiable behaviour' before Isaac Drury on Wednesday, 26 September
1750.[70] However, in an action of equal importance, when faced with the
alternatives of severe sanction or exile, a 'large company of rioters', estimated
at between 40 and 50, chose to become indentured servants and embark on
4 March 1751 for North America rather than accept 'the punishment justly
due their crimes'.[71]

Since a similar tactic had been employed successfully in 1730 to weaken
the Kevan Bail, it was inevitable that the transportation of a still greater
number of rioters in 1751 should have a direct impact on the level of

factional activity in the city. Clashes between the Ormond and Liberty Boys, which showed signs of increasing in the spring of that year, fell away for a time,[72] and when the practice resumed it was at a significantly lower level than it had been a year earlier. This was due primarily to the diminished participation of the Ormond Boys, who virtually disappeared from view for a time, which suggests that they suffered most from the collective loss of confidence among factional activists that seems to have occurred in the winter of 1750–51.[73] The Liberty Boys were more visible, despite the close attention they were afforded by Isaac Drury, who was responsible personally for killing Nolan, the reputed 'head of the Liberty rioters', in June.[74] The onset of the fair season prompted an increase in factional activity, but other than at St James's fair, Donnybrook fair and one other occasion when the Liberty Boys engaged with the Ormond Boys,[75] the Liberty Boys fought variously during the second half of 1751 with the 'County People' at Rathfarnham, in south County Dublin, and, in the most serious sequence of encounters of that year, with a faction known variously as the Blacksmiths or the 'Men of Kilmainham' as a result of which four people died of injuries received and one person was executed.[76] This faction faded from view thereafter, and the rare appearances of the Ormond Boys during 1752, 1753 and 1754 indicated that they too continued to lack spirit and direction.[77] This effectively left the way clear for the Liberty Boys, who emphasised their dominant position by challenging any rivals who appeared on the horizon, but the allure of political and economic protest siphoned off an increasing amount of the energy previously devoted to factional pursuits.

Given the weakness of their main rival, the reliance of the Liberties economically on textiles, and the growth in the public sphere prompted by the Money Bill dispute, it is hardly surprising that the Liberty Boys did not sustain the high level of factional activity they had demonstrated during the late 1740s and early-1750s into the mid- and late-1750s. The difficult political and economic environment was particularly important since it hastened the process of popular politicisation, already manifest during the 1749 by-election, highlighted by the participation in May 1753 of 2,000 residents from the Liberties with 'green boughs' in their hats in a march in support of the patriot stand taken by the earl of Kildare.[78] The involvement of smaller numbers, described explicitly in the reports of such incidents as Liberty Boys, in opposition to the consumption of foreign textiles conformed to a more familiar pattern of activity, but it too deviated from the normal contours of factional activity.[79] The implication that the Liberty Boys now participated in a wider range of forms of collective activity, while adhering to their factional traditions, is confirmed by their engagement during 1752 with the 'buffers' of Finglas, during 1753 with the Stoneybatter mob and the butchers of the Glibb, Thomas Street, during 1754 with the sailors on Lazer's Hill, the butchers of the Glibb, and the Penny Boys of

Smithfield, and at other times with a diversity of more shadowy groups and interests, many of them within their own territory.[80] There might have been more incidents of this kind but for the efforts of Isaac Drury, whose decisive intervention frustrated an attempt to animate rioting in the Liberties in March–April 1753.[81] As a result, the intervals between factional encounters grew progressively longer during the mid-1750s, prompting newspapers to observe that 'there is now no kind of appearance of [factional] rioting throughout the Liberty'. This was not strictly true, as the incidents referred to above, and others such as the riot precipitated by a number of 'idle fellows', who assembled at Donnybrook Fair and sought to invade the Liberties in 1753, attest. However, consistent with the pattern of factional violence demonstrated since the late 1720s, the sharp bursts of activity observable between 1748 and 1752 could not be sustained, and it was followed by a period of quiet.[82]

This lasted for over a decade, though the streets of the capital were seldom free for long from the manifestations of disorder during that time. Moreover, as on previous occasions, the local and sectoral identities that provided much of the rationale for and the sustenance of factional activity proved enduring. It can be identified, for example, in the readiness of 'Liberty rioters' and gangs of butchers from Ormond Market in 1754–5 to battle it out with the watch and the constables in response to aggressive behaviour by the latter, and in the quarrel between journeymen tailors and shoemakers in which several on both side were wounded in April 1756.[83] Both factions continued meanwhile to regard the other with suspicion.[84] This obliged municipal officials to remain alert to ensure that traditional events like Donnybrook fair did not provide the spark that ignited this tinder of hostility, but they were comparatively relaxed.[85] The official position was expressed by the lord lieutenant, the earl of Hartington, when he observed complacently in August 1755 that 'the town is apt to be riotous at this time of the year, [but] I do not apprehend it to have been much more than is usual.'[86] In point of fact, Dublin was more disturbed in 1755 than it had been the previous year and than it was to be during the remainder of the 1750s and early 1760s. However, despite reports of the appearance on the street at night of parties of 'armed rioters', and alarmist accounts of 'great riots' and 'great quarrels', the modest size of the participating groups, the limited character of the exchanges in which they engaged, and their intermittent ocurrence meant that they posed less of a threat to social order than the serried ranks of the city's major factions when they were mobilised. The authorities did not hesitate to commend the public against 'joining in riots and mobs', but so long as reported disturbances, such as that which took place in May 1756 between a soldier and a butcher at Oxmantown Green, did not prompt overtly factional violence, their admonitions commanded little of the attention they had elicited some years earlier when faction was vibrant.[87] The fact that Dublin corporation was more concerned with street robbery than faction fighting in the early 1760s is particularly revealing of how quiet the factional impulse was at this moment.[88]

III

The hiatus in factional activity in Dublin spanning the late 1750s and early 1760s concluded in 1764. The city's main factions – the Ormond Boys and Liberty Boys – had quite different experiences during these years. Based on the absence of reference to them in the press, the Ormond Boys seem effectively not to have functioned as a working faction during this time, though the frequent involvement of small groups of butchers in altercations and exchanges with members of the large city garrison indicates that the appeal of violence remained undiminished. The Liberty Boys maintained a more distinct presence, though they directed their energies, previously devoted to upholding the honour of the faction, increasingly towards popular political protest. The best documented illustration of this is provided by the participation of large number from the Liberties in the riots, prompted by a rumour that an Anglo-Irish union was in contemplation, that disturbed the capital towards the end of 1759. The protests that followed the desertion by Speaker Boyle of the 'patriot' cause three years earlier are equally indicative.[89]

Popular politicisation did not cease as the aftershocks of the Money Bill dispute faded, but the absence of serious economic or political crisis during the late 1750s and early 1760s meant there was more scope for the expression of other aspects of public identity. This had less impact on Catholic interests, in keeping with the greater restrictions on their admission to the public sphere, than it had on Protestant, but the re-emergence in the mid-1760s of the Ormond Boys as a coherent faction was crucial to the survival of a vibrant factional culture in the city. This could not be assumed, not least because the Ormond interest failed to mount convincing resistance to an attack by 'a considerable number of rioters from the tents at the Strand' when they descended on Ormond Market in August 1764.[90] However, there was to be no repetition of this humiliation, and stimulated by the vulnerability experienced by the population of the markets area, a new generation of Ormond Boys gathered.[91] They were sufficiently well organised by the spring of 1765 to be in a position to resume the contest with the Liberty Boys with the object of establishing which was the dominant faction.

The last phase of the struggle that had been pursued intermittently since the mid-1730s by the Liberty and Ormond Boys lasted for some five years. It was thus of longer duration than earlier phases. A number of factors contributed to bring this about, but perhaps the most important was the different manner in which the factions conducted their activities. On previous occasions when the two factions had battled to determine which was strongest, most encounters, other than those at fairs, took place on streets, bridges or on open spaces within the city limits. However, events following the renewal of this struggle in 1748 demonstrated that the lord mayor and sheriffs of the city had the resources and the know how to combat faction in the city, and that their increased appeal to legal sanction gave them a decisive tactical advantage. The defiant attitude of Thady Foy, the Liberty Boy 'captain', who 'behaved most insolently and rudely to the chairman' of the Commission of Oyer and Terminer who sentenced him to be hanged and quartered in 1737 indicates that the willingness to set the law at defiance in pursuit of the right to fight was deeply engrained. This may account for the fact that the encounters that signalled the resumption of 'the diversion of club law' between the Liberty and Ormond boys in late spring and summer of 1765 took place at Oxmantown Green.[92] However, the authorities made it all but impossible for the protagonists to continue by the simple expedient of placing a strong guard on the Liffey bridges. Obliged to challenge the authorities directly, and accept the likelihood of severe sanction, if they wished to continue to fight in convenient central locations, or to identify an alternative public space, the factions seem to have determined on the latter course of action.[93] One possibility, pointed to by an encounter at Dolphin's Barn and Marybone Lane involving an estimated 500 persons in April 1764, was to move to the western outskirts of the city.[94] The attraction of this location was enhanced by the alarm expressed by the 'inhabitants about James Street' when the Ormond and Liberty boys clashed in their neighbourhood on 1 December 1765, and by the interruption by the military of a factional engagement in Kevin Street in 1766. Similar unease, expressed by the St Audeon's parish vestry at the activities of a 'gang' of rioters in that quarter of town, was also a consideration, but it was not until 1767 that a suitable alternative venue was identified.[95] This was Long Lane, a narrow road than ran through the fields separating New Street and Kevan's Port. Along with the nearby fields and Liberty Lane, this was to serve as the epicentre of faction fighting in the city for the next three years (fig. 4).[96]

The use of swords, hangers, fulchions, knives and bludgeons ensured that horrifying injuries (involving the loss of arms, legs, hands, noses and so on) were inflicted every time the Ormond and Liberty Boys met during the late 1760s, which (according to some reports) was 'every Sunday'. Moreover, and in obvious contrast to Donnybrook fair, which was now closely monitored, the authorities showed little inclination to intervene.[97] The ever-vigilant Isaac Drury was the most notable exception, but though he responded to a number of requests for assistance, it was not until early in 1769, when fighting on Long Lane became a matter of public controversy and the inhabitants of Kevin's Port and New Street made their 'annoyance' known, that the authorities responded with any urgency.[98] Beginning on 27 February, a party

5 Map of Newmarket, Weaver's Square, Dolphin's Barn areas, by John Rocque, 1756

of the Newmarket and Poddle guards 'went to the fields between New Street and Kevin's Port, and dispersed a great number of armed rioters' on consecutive Sundays. It proved decisive; fighting did not cease immediately, but deprived of a reliable venue, the devotees of faction were obliged to revert to their old city locations.[99] This too proved unsustainable and organised fighting between the largest, most enduring and best-known factions in the city had all but ceased by the beginning of the 1770s.

3. The changing character of factional riot, 1770–91

The eclipse of the Ormond and Liberty Boys was a turning point in the history of factional activity in Dublin. It did not signal the end of faction *per se*, or indeed of Ormond Market and the Liberties as a source of riot, but the most persistent manifestations of factional activity in Dublin city and environs during the remainder of the century were to be found in the city's outskirts, specifically in the nearby towns and villages, which manifested a degree of attachment to faction that was masked so long as the Ormond and Liberty Boys were active. Purely factional activity diminished appreciably in the city, meanwhile, though the vacuum left by the demise of the Liberty and Ormond Boys was filled for a time by a plethora of largely short-lived factions, whose influence rarely extended far beyond the locality in which they had originated. However, the factional disposition proved enduring, and it was visible once more in the early 1790s when, as a result of unease among those in the textile sector with new work practices, there was a brief surge in factional activity instigated by disgruntled journeymen. Paradoxically, their actions attested at once to the strength of the legacy of faction and to the fact that it had been superseded in the city by a more conventional form of industrial protest.

The negative consequences for faction of the incapacity of both the Liberty and Ormond Boys to negotiate the challenge posed by the authorities' interdiction of the use of Long Lane and environs as a venue for fighting was reinforced by the intensification of the ongoing campaign to improve the behaviour and conduct of the population. This was underlined in October 1769 when the lord mayor of Dublin, Thomas Blackall, authorised a proclamation in which he prioritised Sabbath observance and the discouragement of 'drunkenness, profaneness and immorality'.[1] The tighter regulation of fairs like Donnybrook accorded with this improving vision, and it is significant that the decline in factional violence at this and other fairs prompted persistent calls in the 1780s for a sustained effort to limit alcohol consumption on such occasions since drinking was widely perceived as one of the primary causes of the substantial number of murderous 'quarrels' and assaults that took place at these gatherings.[2] This proved only partially successful, but it complemented the narrowing of the environment in which faction fighting could now take place, which inevitably had a visible impact on the pattern of factional behaviour in Dublin and environs.

This was not always obvious in the early 1770s as the downturn in commercial activity, which hit the textile sector hard, encouraged disgruntled operatives to assemble in substantial mobs both to promote the wearing of Irish manufactures and to target competitive fabrics (muslins and nanquins particularly) for destruction.[3] Attacks on the enterprises of woollen drapers and on individuals wearing rival fabrics were also a feature of this campaign, as they had been previously when journeymen straddled membership of Liberty factions and workers combinations. The involvement of the Liberty Lighthorse, a shadowy group which comprised young men who had once been embraced within the Liberty Boys, represented a direct link with the earlier world. They responded to the changed economic climate and to what they described as 'the death of their loom' by 'levying contributions' from shopkeepers, weavers and by rescuing men taken up for rioting, as a result of which they gravitated towards the quasi-criminal behaviour of combinations and the gang culture that flourished in Dublin in the 1770s and afterwards.[4] A link can also be made between the Liberty Boys and the Liberty Lads, a short-lived body who clashed for a time in the mid-1770s with members of the Green Regiment.[5] However, the most crucial fact about faction on the south side of the Liffey in the aftermath of the dissolution of the Liberty Boys was its weakness.

This is manifest when one seeks to identify the factional interests that were active in this area of the city during the 1770s. One notable development was the emergence of the Dolphin Barn Boys and Marybone Lane Boys as factional interests in their own right (fig. 5). They fought each other and the 'rioters of New Street' intermittently during the 1770s, but made little impression outside their locality.[6] They may have had some relationship with the 'vagabonds known by the name of buffers' who colonised the Long Lane area in the mid-1770s. However, apart from an occasional 'May bush' riot, and sporadic activity by occupational groups like the draymen of St James' brewery, who pursued a dispute with the Newgate guard in 1779, the students of Trinity College who sustained their intermittently violent relationship with the city watch, and ephemeral groups like the 'mariners', whose conduct bore closer resemblance to that of a criminal gang than a fully fledged faction, there was little identifiable factional fighting in the southern parts of the city.[7] This may explain why the 'New Street party', which survived longer than most, fought on occasions in the fields about Rathgar with the Harold's Cross mob and their 'mountain neighbours'; it seems that they had to reach out to the factions in the countryside to the south of the city for rivals.[8]

The situation on the north side of the city was more competitive, as a significant number of factions named after their place of origin emerged out of the ashes of the Ormond Boys. Like their southern equivalents few proved durable, though the Cross Lane Boys survived longer than most, and demonstrated, through their readiness to engage with the New Market Boys of the south side in 1776 and by their activities on the Drumcondra Road that, they possessed considerable ambition.[9] Others groups, which also took their name from a thoroughfare – Liffey Street, Henry Street, Marlborough Street, the North Strand – and who were as likely as not to fight on the streets or at such open spaces as the Little Green or Oxmantown Green (more rarely), enjoyed a shorter existence, usually because the local population did not hesitate to alert the city sheriff or to invite the watch to intervene and put an end to such lawless behaviour as these factions engaged in.[10]

Because of the refusal of parish and local residential communities in the north city to indulge such behaviour, the focus of factional activity was forced outwards to newly-emerging communities on the main routes into the capital. In places such as Stoneybatter, where faction fighting had already established deep roots, the determination of local interests to preserve the traditional customs associated with collecting and erecting a May bush brought them into direct conflict with the authorities who were committed to eradicate the practice because of its factional associations. The most serious encounters involved the military and 'the mob of Stoneybatter', who engaged in a number of sharp disputes between March and May 1773, but the enthusiasm for May bushes was such that clashes between factions carrying May poles and the authorities were also reported during the 1770s on Prussia Street, Dorset Street and in St Mary's parish, and, as late as 1798, at Harold's Cross.[11] Some of these involved rural factional interests drawn to fight in the city, such as the Maymen of Glasnevin who fought the Stoneybatter mob at Cross Lane in 1771; others chose the occasion of a traditional fair such as Palmerstown to engage in a trial of strength. The more enduring were the factions that emerged in the 'villages' of Drumcondra, Glasnevin, Santry, Finglas and Glassmanogue. They fought with each other (in some cases repeatedly) during the 1770s and 1780s at various northside locations, notably off the North Circular Road in 1789 and 1791, when the Drumcondra faction met that of neighbouring Glasnevin. A year earlier at Drumcondra, the 'barbarous spirit of idle contention for the ragged pride of villages and districts' prompted a meeting of 'Finglas and Glasnevin … to decide a match of club law with those of Santry and Drumcondra', and a 'scene of worse than savage barbarity presented nothing but blood, oaths, blasphemy and execrations'.[12] At other times, the Glasnevin mob, the Drumcondra gardeners and the Glassmanogue rioters assembled on Sundays during the summer months and fought whoever was willing to meet them.[13]

While this suggests that the decline in faction fighting identifiable in the city of Dublin was at least partly compensated for by the vigour of the practice in the outlying towns and villages, and among smaller niche communities, the reality was that the critical mass of artisans who resided in the parishes on the northern and southern sides of the Liffey had little interest in pursuing a purely factional agenda. This was most evident in the Liberties, whose population was drawn into increasingly politicised activity through their participation in combinations as well as in the campaigns for free trade, legislative independence and parliamentary reform, which dominated Irish politics between 1778 and 1785. This latter involvement can be traced to the campaign (in itself a continuation of a cause agitated intermittently since the 1730s) for increased home consumption pursued in the difficult economic climate of the early 1770s against the competitors of the Liberties textile producers. This climaxed in the non-consumption and non-importation campaigns that were pursued in the late 1770s in the course of which 'riotous' Liberty mobs paraded the streets seeking out 'English goods' for destruction. Sustained primarily by journeymen artisans, it represented the more volatile fringe aspect of a popular campaign that engendered widespread support as evidenced by the participation of thousands from the Liberties in protests outside the houses of parliament in November 1779, November 1783 and April 1784, as well as by the proliferation of combinations in the last quarter of the century.[14]

Meanwhile, spurred on by a deterioration in civilian-military relations hastened by the intensification of military activity arising out of the augmented military establishment and the implications of war in America, the long simmering animosity between the butchers of Ormond market and the army garrison boiled over. The starting point can be traced to a series of attacks on individual soldiers in the winter of 1773–4, which escalated in the course of the latter year into a campaign of houghing that lasted, with interruptions, until the mid-1780s. While the Dublin garrison would have been better served probably if the soldiers under its command had maintained their discipline and responded in a more controlled way to these attacks, the fact that they allowed themselves to be provoked into reprisals served only to exacerbate public resentment in the Ormond market, and to intensify the resulting animosity. It served also to perpetuate the distinctive group identity among the butchers that had sustained the Ormond Boys, though it is noteworthy that rather than promoting the reconstitution of the Ormond Boy faction it had led to more obvious criminal activity by 'gangs' of butchers from the late 1770s.[15] Neither this nor the targeting of soldiers for attack possessed the obvious political character of the protests in which the Liberty Boys engaged, but by sustaining the group identity of the butchers it acted as a counterweight to the desire of respectable society to eradicate the factional impulse.

This seemed a likely prospect in the mid-1780s, as, in the continued absence of faction fighting on the streets of the city, it was perceived in some quarters that the Ormond and Liberty Boys, no less than the Cavan Bail, were but an historical memory. Not everybody was so sure, and the very mention of the Liberty Boys was sufficient to cause unease.[16] This was an understandable response, for though there was no occasion in which organised factional groups answering to the names Liberty or Ormond Boys took to the streets in the 1780s, the series of 'dreadful riot[s]' that took place on Ormond Quay between butchers and tailors in September 1782, in which one man was killed and several seriously wounded, inevitably evoked vivid memories of past factional encounters.[17] The active participation of journeymen from the Liberties in the protests in support of protecting duties, and in the tarring and feathering campaign waged against hesitant employers and textile imported in 1784 did likewise, not least because it reminded both the authorities and the respectable of the volatility of the 'mob' in these areas.[18] In practice, the impact of popular politicisation and the intensification of combinations among journeymen, symbolised by the continuing activity of the Liberty Lighthorse in 'levying' contributions from 'manufacturers' meant that most such activity had an economic rather than a factional purpose,[19] though the factional impulse proved resilient in the teeth of intensified efforts in the 1780s to promote a reformation in manners. The most significant institutional manifestation of this reformative tendency was the establishment in 1786 of a Dublin police force, which was conceived of as a response to the 'popular licentiousness' that gripped the Liberties in 1784, but the intensification of the campaigns against alcohol, gambling, bull baiting and other controversial popular recreational practices that were linked intimately with riotous behaviour and the profanation of the Sabbath was no less indicative.[20]

Against this background, it was understandable why the surge in rioting that took place in the early 1790s should be seen in many quarters as a return to the bad old days of rampant faction. It is these events that inform John Edward Walsh's influential description of the Ormond and Liberty Boys, though the case in favour of attributing them to these factions is weak. This is not to claim that the rioting that took place in the early 1790s did not possess a factional dimension, or that Walsh and others who made the attribution were wilfully and egregiously in error when their main mistake was to assume that what they witnessed in 1790 was representative of what had gone before.[21] In fact, though this phase of disorder was attributed by some contemporaries to the heightened tensions generated by the elections held in Dublin city and county in 1790, the initial 'affrays', which took place in the Liberties, involved 'working men' in rival and competitive trades. They were, in other words, a product in the first instance of a difficult industrial relations' climate ultimately attributable to the destabilising impact of the adoption of new industrial technology that exerted downwards pressure on wages and employment rather than political or factional rivalry.[22] However, they had hardly been brought under control when a misunderstanding between the tailors of the Liberties and the butchers of Ormond Market on Sunday 9 May precipitated a riot that seemed to herald a return to the old days of faction fighting.

Sparked off by the objection expressed by 'a number of butchers' to the disciplining by some tailors of a man for working under price, it escalated into a five-hour riot redolent of the 1740s, as the two interests battled to take control of the city bridges 'as a post of honour'. Two men were killed as each contrived to gain the upper hand, but as neither was deemed to have achieved an identifiable advantage, it was agreed that this was 'a drawn battle', and that the contest should be resumed the next day. Because this was a predictable factional response, and because the exchanges that took place on Monday, 10 May, resulted in two more deaths, and gave rise to acute feelings of 'terror and danger' among those of the citizenry that witnessed the riot, it was hardly surprising that many concluded ominously that factional violence had returned to the city streets. In fact, this was not to be the case. Having reassembled on the morning of Tuesday, 11 May, in large numbers with swords and other weapons, to resume their trial of strength it was agreed on the suggestion of the butchers' leaders to effect a 'reconciliation' and conclude hostilities.[23]

In practice, though nobody realised it at the time, this represented the last kick of a tradition of urban faction fighting that dated back to the 1720s, for when rioting resumed in the Liberties and environs later in 1790, and continued at intervals into 1791 and 1792, the participants were rival textile operatives. Their exchanges continued to echo aspects of the tradition of faction fighting in that they chose on occasion to meet at pre-determined locations – Dolphin's Barn notably – to 'try their mutual strength'. The involvement of the Liberty Lighthorse was another echo of the tradition of faction fighting, but since they were now a fully-fledged part of the aggressive strand of combinations that had developed since the 1770s, these events have more to do with this phenomenon than the now anachronistic tradition of urban faction.[24]

Conclusion

Though there is much about the operation and motivation[1] of faction in 18th-century Dublin that eludes recovery, the closeness of the relationship of the Liberty Boys with journeymen societies and with the combinations they forged in support of improved wages and conditions indicates that the activities of the main urban factions cannot be dismissed as simple hooliganism. It is doubtless the case that involvement with a faction provided some who found fighting agreeable with an ideal opportunity to express that instinct, but for a majority participation was neither the mindless nor aimless exercise its contemporary critics proclaimed. The main factions that can be identified as operating in Dublin city and county in the 18th century were named after the locations from which they emanated, which is illustrative of their identification with their place of origin and of their pride in the communities that sustained them. This was reinforced by a strong competitive aspect and by a readiness to employ force to prevail over rivals that was more developed in young men than in those of older age. This may assist in comprehending the intermittent nature of factional disorder, and its location in growing communities, but if the population profile and the cycle of community development is critical to any attempt to make sense of faction activity in Dublin in the 18th century, the indulgent attitude demonstrated to violence within these communities must also be acknowledged. Both these points can be identified most readily with respect of those areas in which mass artisan housing was put in place in the early and mid-18th century, but it was subsequently manifest, when the tide had turned against faction in the city, in the fast growing villages on the main roads to the capital.

As this implies, factions were not the irrational purveyors of the motiveless violence of legend. Most factions possessed leaders, some of who are known by name, who were figures of authority within their communities. It is not clear precisely what role or roles they performed in directing faction, but since the Ormond and Liberty Boys entered into alliances against common enemies and agreed truces on occasions, there is good reason for assuming that they determined strategy, conveyed challenges, chose when and where fights would take place, how they would be conducted, led their factions into battle, and determined other aspects of the culture of 'Club law' that was integral to the identity and experience of so many of the lower order residents of the teeming commercial heartlands of 18th-century Dublin. The impression this gives of bodies guided by principles and precepts different to, and perhaps incompatible with, those of respectable society and officialdom is sustained by the fact that the activities of the Liberty Boys gradually gave way to politicisation and to combination, which addressed popular needs in a more conventional and comprehensible manner. This process took longer where the strength of local identity did not have to compete as closely with the force of politicisation, with the result that the combination of local, personal and atavistic differences that sustained faction survive for considerably longer in other locations.

As home to the most varied and most numerous urban communities in the kingdom, it was inevitable that Dublin should sustain a factional culture different from elsewhere, but it was not so different that some parallels cannot be drawn with Cork, which was the only major urban centre to emulate Dublin in sustaining a number of factional bodies over a sustained length of time. From the initial recording of their engagement in May 1753 in a contest to determine who would 'bring home' the May bush, which was the primary focus of their factional activities, the Blackpool and Fair Lane Boys, sustained a rivalry in the city that lasted nearly thirty years. Together with the Blarney Lane Boys, these factions assembled 'to the number of two thousand and upwards' when they were at their most active in the 1760s and early 1770s. However, though the main factions in Cork were able for a time to defy the efforts of the authorities to dissuade them from their 'barbarous and savage custom of fighting', they too were unable to withstand the intensified demand for respectability that took hold in the last quarter of the eighteenth century.[2] Since this posed a serious challenge to respectable practices such as duelling,[3] it is hardly surprising that faction proved vulnerable when the circumstances that had brought it into being also changed. By the end of the 18th century, factional violence was a rarity in the main cities of Dublin and Cork, where once it had been commonplace. Its future lay in the countryside where the distinctive sense of community and requisite demographic structure coexisted with the social and cultural assumptions necessary to sustain the practice of factional rioting for several more generations.

Notes

ABBREVIATIONS

DC	Dublin Chronicle	FLJ	Finn's Leinster Journal
DCt	Dublin Courant	HDIN	Harding's Dublin Impartial Newsletter
DDA	Dublin Daily Advertizer	HJ	Hibernian Journal
DDP	Dublin Daily Post	NDP	Needham's Dublin Postman
DI	Dublin Intelligence	NAI	National Archives of Ireland
DEP	Dublin Evening Post	OED	Oxford English Dictionary
DG	Dublin Gazette	PO	Pue's Occurrences
DM	Dublin Mercury	PRONI	Public Record Office of Northern Ireland
DN	Dublin Newsletter	RIA	Royal Irish Academy
DP	Dublin Postman	TCD	Trinity College Dublin
DWJ	Dublin Weekly Journal	UCD	University College Dublin
EN	Esdall's Newsletter	VEP	Volunteer Evening Post
FJ	Freeman's Journal	WN	Whalley's Newsletter
FDJ	Faulkner's Dublin Journal		

INTRODUCTION

1 See, for example *Irish Roots*, no. 7 (1993) where it is stated 'faction fighting was a phenomenon unique to nineteenth-century Ireland'.

2 J. Kelly, 'The abduction of women of fortune in eighteenth-century Ireland', *Eighteenth-Century Ireland*, 9 (1994), pp 7–43.

3 For an excellent overview see D. Dickson, *Ireland 1660–1800: new foundations* (2nd ed., Dublin, 2000), pp 147–51.

4 P. Fagan, 'The Dublin Catholic mob (1700–1750)', *Eighteenth-Century Ireland*, 4 (1989), pp 133–42; idem, *The second city: Dublin, 1700–60* (Dublin, 1986), pp 46–9; S. Murphy, 'Municipal politics and popular disturbances, 1660–1800' in A. Cosgrave (ed.), *Dublin through the ages* (Dublin, 1988), p. 86.

5 Murphy, 'Popular disturbances', p. 82; Fagan, 'Dublin Catholic mob', p. 140.

6 P. O'Donnell, *The Irish faction fighters in the nineteenth century* (Dublin, 1975).

7 [J.E. Walsh], *Sketches of Ireland sixty years ago* (Dublin, 1847), p. 3

8 See, for example, J.S. Donnelly, 'The Rightboys, 1785–88', *Studia Hibernica*, 17 & 18 (1977–8), pp 120–202.

9 *DWJ*, 17 Sept. 1748. My italics.

10 S. Ní Chinneide, 'Coquebert de Montbret's impressions of Galway city and county in … 1791', *Journal of the Galway Archaeological and Historical Society*, 25 (1952), pp 3–4; *HJ*, 14 July 1780; 14, 28 Aug. 1782; *FJ*, 12 Apr. 1785, 14 Feb. 1786, 27 June 1789; *FLJ*, 13, 16 Jan. 1773, 5 Sept. 1778; *DC*, 11 Oct. 1787, 9 Nov. 1790.

11 *Munster Journal*, 23 Aug. 1779; *FJ*, 29 Apr. 1775; *HJ*, 2 Aug. 1780; *DC*, 14 Aug. 1787.

12 *PO*, 8 May 1753; *FJ*, 5 May 1764, 28 Sept. 1765, 11 Apr. 1772; *HJ*, 13 Apr., 11 May 1772, 16 June 1773; *FLJ*, 8 May 1773; F.H. Tuckey, *The county and city of Cork Remembrancer* (Cork, 1837), pp 140–1, 151, 153, 161.

13 J.D. Herbert, *Irish varieties for the last fifty years* (London, 1836), p. 84.

14 *PO*, 8 May 1753; *FJ*, 5 May. 1764; *HJ*, 11 May 1772.

15 H.P.R. Finberg, 'Local history' in idem (ed.), *Approaches to history* (London,

1962), p. 121; J.D. Marshall, *The tyranny of the discrete: a discussion of the problem of local history in England* (Aldershot, 1997), pp 64–6.

I. THE KEVAN BAIL AND THE COMMENCEMENT OF FACTIONAL DISORDER

1 D. Dickson, 'The demographic implications of Dublin's growth, 1650–1850' in R. Lawton and R. Lee (eds), *Urban population development in western Europe* (Liverpool, 1989); P. Fagan, 'The population of Dublin in the eighteenth century', *Eighteenth-Century Ireland,* 6 (1991), pp 121–56.

2 F.R. Falkiner, *The foundation of the hospital and free school of King Charles II* (Dublin, 1906), pp 43–4; N.T. Burke. 'Dublin 1600–1800: a study in urban morpho-genesis' (Ph.D. thesis, TCD, 1972); B. Twomey '"To the honour, beauty and profit of the citty": the suburb of Smithfield and the parish of St Paul, Dublin 1698–1750' (Ph.D. thesis, NUI, Maynooth, 2004), pp 112–13, appendix vi.

3 F.E. Ball, *Judges in Ireland* (2 vols, London, 1922), i, 349–50; Sir J. Gilbert (ed.), *Calendar of ancient records of Dublin* (19 vols, Dublin, 1889–1943), v, 237–8.

4 W. Harris, *The history and antiquities of the city of Dublin* (Dublin, 1766), pp 102, 473; Gilbert (ed.), *Ancient records*, vi, 176; Twomey, op. cit., p. 113; E. Sheridan, 'Designing the capital, 1660–1800' in J. Brady and A. Simms (eds), *Dublin through space and time* (Dublin, 2001), pp 82–5, 87.

5 Gilbert (ed.), *Ancient records*, v, 603–8, vi, 67–70, 582–605.

6 Ibid., v, 313–15, 603–8; vi, 9, 67–70, 399–400, 470; ix, 58; Charles Brooking, *A map of the city and suburbs of Dublin* (Dublin 1728, reprinted, 1983).

7 See Sheridan, 'Designing the capital', figs 23, 38.

8 Gilbert (ed.), *Ancient Records*, v, 322–3, 341–2; vi, 78, 85–6, 470.

9 Ibid., vi, 579; vii, 577; S. Lewis, *A topographical dictionary of Ireland* (2 vols, London, 1837), ii, 556.

10 Gilbert (ed.), *Ancient records*, vii, 577.

11 Ibid., v, 417.

12 Ibid., vi, 224.

13 NAI, Calendar of presentments, ff 96, 98, 99, 101, 102, 103, 104, 106; Calendar of miscellaneous letters and papers, 1760–89, f. 2.

14 See J. Kelly, 'Commemoration and Protestant identity in Ireland, 1660–1800', *Proceedings of the Royal Irish Academy* 94 C (1994), pp 25–52.

15 *FDJ*, 3 Dec. 1726, 11 Oct. 1729, 2 Dec. 1732.

16 *FDJ*, 12 Jan. 1734.

17 *PO*, 21 Apr. 1733; *DEP*, 21 Apr. 1733.

18 Petition of minister, church wardens and parishioners of St Werburgh to Archbishop King, June 1715 (NAI, Irish Correspondence, 1697–1798, Ms. 2446 f. 171).

19 J.J. Webb, *The guilds of Dublin* (Dublin, 1929), chapter 7; J. Hill, *From patriots to unionists: Dublin's civic politics and Irish Protestant patriotism, 1660–1800* (Oxford, 1997), pp 40–1; *NDP*, 10 Jan. 1725.

20 Winchelsea and Galway to Vernon, 4 Mar. 1699 (NAI, Irish Correspondence, MS 2447 ff 54–5).

21 T.C. Barnard, *A new anatomy of Ireland* (London, 2002), p. 284.

22 Ibid., p. 287.

23 NAI, Calendar of miscellaneous letters and papers prior to 1760, ff 164, 170, 176.

24 *DI*, 29 July 1729, 9 June 1731; *HDIN*, 28 July 1724; *FDJ*, 15 June, 26 Oct. 1734.

25 *FDJ*, 26 July 1726, 28 July 1739, 27 July 1734, 18 June 1737; *DWJ*, 31 July 1731; *DG*, 25 July 1732.

26 J. Kelly, 'Harvests and hardship: famine and scarcity in Ireland in the late 1720s', *Studia Hibernica* 26 (1991–2), pp 65–106; *DWJ*, 22 Aug. 1730; *DI*, 16, 23 June, 14 July 1731.

27 *DG*, 24 July 1731, 28 July 1733.

28 *DI*, 16 June 1731.

29 *DI*, 10 June 1729.

30 *NDP*, 2 Sept. 1724.

31 J. Kelly, *Gallows speeches from eighteenth-century Ireland* (Dublin, 2002).

32 *A full and true account of a furious and bloody battle which was fought on Sunday the 28th Day of February, 1724–5 in Oxmantown Green, between the mob of the*

town and the standing army (Dublin, 1725).

33 *DP*, 15 Nov. 1716; *Whitehall Gazette*, 14 Aug. 1727; *NDP*, 16 Aug. 1727; *DI*, 31 Aug. 1728.

34 Fagan, *The second city*, pp 124–5; idem, 'The Dublin Catholic mob', pp 135–6.

35 King to Stearne, 17 May, King to Delasay, 2 June, King to Hamilton, 27 May 1715 (TCD, King Papers, Ms 2536 ff 282, 308, 301).

36 *NDP*, 11 June; *DI*, 13, 17 June 1724.

37 *DI*, 11 June 1726; *DWJ*, 11 June 1726; Boulter to Newcastle, 11 June 1726 in *Letters written by Hugh Boulter DD* (2 vols, Dublin, 1770), i, 65–6.

38 *DI*, 10 June 1727.

39 *DI*, 25 Aug., 22 Sept 1724; *A full and true account of a furious and bloody battle, 1724–5.*

40 *DI*, 28 Dec. 1728; *WN*, 21, 24 Mar. 1722.

41 Kelly, 'Harvests and hardship', pp 88–9; G. MacNamara, 'The mayoralty dispute in Dublin, 1707–14' (UCD, MA thesis, 1982); *DI*, 8 Sept. 1724; E.P. Thompson, 'The moral economy of the crowd' in idem, *Customs in common: studies in traditional popular culture* (London, 1993).

42 A.C. Elias (ed.), *Memoirs of Letitia Pilkington* (2 vols, Athens, Georgia, 1997), p. 716; *DI*, 6 Apr. 1729.

43 *DI*, 8 Apr. 1729; S.J. Connolly, *Religion, law and power: the making of Protestant Ireland, 1660–1760* (Oxford, 1992), p. 213.

44 *DI*, 12 Apr. 1729.

45 *DI*, 8, 26 Apr., 10 June 1729.

46 *DI*, 14 June 1729.

47 The text of the proclamation can be consulted in Gilbert (ed.), *Ancient records*, viii, 511–4 and *DG*, 24 June 1729.

48 *DI*, 24 June 1729; *DWJ*, 13 Nov. 1731.

49 *FDJ*, 23 August. 1729.

50 *DI*, 24 June, 20 Aug. 1729; Gilbert (ed.), *Ancient records*, vii, 465.

51 Gilbert (ed.), *Ancient records*, vii, 472; *DWJ*, 23 Aug. 1729; *DI*, 19 July, 20 Aug. 1729.

52 Gilbert (ed.), *Ancient records*, vii, 465; *DG*, 26 Aug. 1729; *DI*, 26 Aug. 1729. It is noteworthy that Dublin Corporation renewed its proclamation again in February 1730 (Gilbert, op cit., vii, 481–2).

53 *DWJ*, 23, 30 Aug., 25 Oct., 6 Dec.; *DI*, 24 June; *FDJ*, 23, 26 Aug., 16 Sept.; *DG*, 27 Sept. 1729.

54 *FDJ*, 7 Feb. 1730.

55 *DI*, 24 June, 29 July 1729.

56 *DG*, 23 Sept. 1729; Gilbert (ed.), *Ancient records*, xi, 527–33; N. Garnham, 'The short career of Paul Farrell: a brief consideration of law enforcement in eighteenth-century Dublin', *Eighteenth-Century Ireland* 11 (1996), pp 46–52; 10 George I, chap 3; *FDJ*, 14 June, 6, 23 Sept. 1729, 21 Nov. 1732.

57 *FDJ*, 7 July 1730; *DI*, 8 Mar. 1731.

58 *FDJ*, 10 Feb., 14 Mar., 4 July 1730; Affidavit of Mathew Menkins, 30 Nov. 1730 (NAI, Calendar of Presentments, f. 88).

59 *DI*, 23 Dec. 1730.

60 *DWJ*, 14 Mar., 31 Oct.; *FDJ*, 7 July 1730.

2. THE ORMOND AND LIBERTY BOYS, 1730–70

1 *PO*, 21 Mar., 19 Aug.; *FDJ*, 2 May 1732.

2 Description of Dublin, 1732 in Gilbert (ed.), *Ancient records*, x, 525.

3 *DG*, 18 Nov. 1729; *FDJ*, 2 Jan. 1731; *DI*, 17, 26 Apr., 3, 5 May, 23 June 1731; *PO*, 18 Nov. 1732.

4 *DI*, 17, 26 Apr. 1731; *A full and true account of a furious and bloody battle*; Elias (ed.), *Pilkington's Memoirs*, p. 323.

5 *DI*, 18 Nov. 1729, 31 Jan. 1730; *DG*, 18 Nov. 1729.

6 *DI*, 26 Apr. 1731; see also *DG*, 18 Nov. 1729.

7 *DWJ*, 13 Mar. 1730, 24 Apr. 1731; *DI*, 5 May, 9, 23 June 1731; *DEP*, 8 July 1732; *DG*, 27 Feb. 1733.

8 *FDJ*, 27 July, 17 Aug. 1731; *DI*, 30 Aug. 1731.

9 Monck Mason Papers, Gilbert Library cited in Fagan, 'The Dublin Catholic mob', p 141.

10 *PO*, 22 Feb., 13 Mar. 1732; *DI*, 9, 16 Mar., 24, 26 Apr.; *DWJ*, 13, 19 Mar. 1731; Bishop Robert Clayton to his wife, 17 Apr. 1731 (Yale University, Beinecke Library, Osborn Collection, Sundon letterbook ff 114–5).

11 *FDJ*, 4 July 1730, 24, 27 Aug. 1734;
    DEP, 24, 27 Aug. 1734; *DG*, 27 Aug.
    1734; *PO*, 24 Aug 1734; Garnham, 'The
    short career of Paul Farrell', pp 46–52.

12 *DI*, 16 June 1731; *FDJ*, 13 Nov. 1731, 9
    July 1734, 24 May 1735; *DEP*, 16 Dec.
    1732, 18 May 1734, 27 Sept. 1735; C.
    Fabricant, *Swift's landscape* (London,
    1982), p. 244; Fagan, *The second city*, pp
    49–50; Gilbert (ed.), *Ancient records*, viii,
    176–7; *PO*, 14 June 1735.

13 *DEP*, 8 July 1732, 5 May 1733.

14 *DEP*, 8 May; *FDJ*, 5 May 1733.

15 See Herbert, *Irish varieties*, p. 83.

16 *DEP*, 24 Aug. 1734. The term Liberty
    Boys had achieved popular currency by
    1735 (*DEP*, 27 May 1735).

17 *DEP*, 24 Aug. 1734; for some discussion
    of this point see Fagan, 'The Dublin
    Catholic mob', p. 139; it is significant
    that other papers simply referred to 'the
    mob' (*PO*, 24 Aug. 1734).

18 *FDJ*, 16 Apr., 7 June 1748.

19 *FDJ*, 26 Apr. 1734.

20 *FDJ*, 30 Apr., 7 Sept., 29 Oct. 1734

21 *FDJ*, 16 Apr. 1734; *DEP*, 16 Nov. 1734;
    DG, 6 May, 10 June 1735.

22 *DEP*, 27 May, 24, 28 June, 8, 12, 29 July,
    11, 15 Nov 1735.

23 *DG*, 7 Feb.; *PO*, 3 June 1736.

24 *DEP*, 10 June 1735, 1 May 1736; *FDJ*,
    21 July 1739; Gilbert (ed.), *Ancient
    records*, viii, 291, 315–6.

25 *DG*, 13 June; *PO*, 15 June 1736.

26 *DG*, 31 July; *DDA*, 7 Oct. 1736.

27 *DEP*, 27 May 1735.

28 *DDA*, 7 Oct.; *DG*, 4 Dec.; *FDJ*,
    30 Nov. 1736.

29 *DG*, 4 Dec. 1736, 26 July, 16 Aug. 1737;
    PO, 26 July, 13 Aug.; *DN*, 26, 30 July,
    13, 18 Aug.; *DDA*, 18 Aug. 1737.

30 *DG*, 20 Aug. 1737.

31 *DDA*, 18 Aug. 1737.

32 *DN*, 20 Aug. 1737.

33 *DN*, 20 Sept. 1737; Gilbert (ed.), *Ancient
    records*, viii, 263.

34 *DG*, 3 Sept., 1, 15 Nov. 1737.

35 *DN*, 6 Sept.; *DG*, 24 Sept 1737.

36 Gilbert (ed.), *Ancient records*, viii, 291,
    315–16, 354–5; *DN*, 29 July 1738.

37 *DN*, 25 Apr.; *DG*, 25 Apr. 1738.

38 *DN*, 27 May; *DG*, 27 May; *PO*, 27 May
    1738.

39 *DN*, 11 July 1738; J. Kelly, 'Capital
    punishment in eighteenth-century
    Ireland' in S. Soupel (ed.), *Crime et
    chatiment dans les Isles Britanniques au
    dix-huitieme siecle* (Paris and Moscow,
    2001), pp 155–72.

40 *DDP*, 12 Feb., 27 Mar., 27 Aug. 1739;
    FDJ, 4 Oct. 1748.

41 Murphy, 'Municipal politics and
    popular disturbances', p. 82; V. Morley,
    *Irish opinion and the American revolution,
    1760–1783* (Cambridge, 2002), pp 90–1;
    N. Garnham, *The courts, crime and the
    criminal law in Ireland, 1692–1760*
    (Dublin, 1996), p. 200.

42 *PO*, 6 Sept. 1748.

43 J. Kelly, 'Commemoration and
    Protestant identity', pp 90–1; *DDP*,
    28 July 1739.

44 *DG*, 26 May 1741.

45 *FDJ*, 2 Oct. 1736; *DG*, 20 Feb.; *DDP*,
    2 May, 16, 27 Aug.; 3 Sept.; *PO*, 28 Aug.
    1739.

46 *DDP*, 19 Feb., 27 May; *DN*, 27 Feb.,
    27 May, 6 Sept.; *PO*, 27 May.; *DG*,
    6 Sept. 1740.

47 *DG*, 7 June 1740; Gilbert (ed.), *Ancient
    records*, viii, 374–5.

48 *DN*, 18 Aug. 1741, 27 July 1742; *PO*, 29
    Mar., 13 Aug., 31 Dec. 1743.

49 Gilbert (ed.), *Ancient records*, ix, 67; *PO*,
    11 Feb., 8 Aug.; *FDJ*, 11 Feb. 1747.

50 *DCt*, 2 Oct. 1750.

51 *FDJ*, 7, 11 June, 16 Aug. 1748.

52 *DCt*, 16 Feb. 1748.

53 *DWJ*, 16 Apr., 11 June; *PO*, 7, 11 June;
    DCt, 7, 11 June; *FDJ*, 16 Apr., 7 June
    1748.

54 *FDJ*, 11 June 1748; Murphy, 'Municipal
    politics', p. 83; J. Brady (ed.), *Catholics in
    the eighteenth-century press* (Maynooth,
    1966), p. 76.

55 *DCt*, 9, 16 Aug.; *FDJ*, 16 Aug. 1748.

56 *PO*, 13 Aug.; *DCt*, 13 Aug.; *FDJ*, 4 Oct.
    1748; Fagan, *The second city*, pp 46–7.

57 *DCt*, 13 Aug. 1748

58 *DCt*, 6, 13, 20, 27 Sept., 1 Oct; *PO*, 6,
    24 Sept., 1 Oct.; *DWJ*, 17 Sept., 1 Oct.;
    FDJ, 6, 20, 24 Sept. 1748.

59 *DG*, 20 Feb. 1739, 2 Sept. 1740; *DCt*, 2
    Oct. 1750; *PO*, 24 Sept. 1751; Elias
    (ed.), *Pilkington's memoirs*, p. 323;
    Herbert, *Irish varieties*, p. 83; the

dictionary definition of a 'falchion', which was also spelled fauchion and falcheon, is broad bladed sword (*OED*).

60 *DCt*, 4 Oct.; *PO*, 4 Oct.; *FDJ*, 4 Oct. 1748; Brady (ed.), *Catholics in the press*, p. 76.

61 *FDJ*, 4, 8, 11 Oct.; *DCt*, 11, 25 Oct.; *PO*, 11 Oct.; *DWJ*, 15 Oct. 1748.

62 *FDJ*, 18 Oct. 1748; Murphy, 'Municipal politics', p. 84.

63 *DCt*, 16 Dec. 1748, 1 Apr., 2 May; *DWJ*, 12 Aug. 1749; Gilbert (ed.), *Ancient records*, ix, 297–8.

64 Murphy, 'Municipal politics', pp 84–5; *DCt*, 24 Oct. 1749.

65 *DCt*, 24 Oct. 1749.

66 *DWJ*, 10 Feb, 2 June; *DCt*, 26 May 1750.

67 Murphy, 'Municipal politics', p. 86; *FDJ*, 3, 7 Apr.; *DCt*, 15, 19 May 1750.

68 *FDJ*, 10, 17 Apr., 9 June; *DWJ*, 14 Apr. 1750. The Privy Council offered a £50 reward for the apprehension of 'each of the first five persons who shall be found guilty' (*EN*, 6 June 1750).

69 *FDJ*, 7 Apr., 28 Aug., 25 Sept., 18 Oct.; *DCt*, 25 Sept., 2 Oct., 3, 27 Nov. 1750, 1 Jan. 1751; *EN*, 29 Aug.; *DWJ*, 6 Oct., 3 Nov. 1750.

70 *DCt*, 29 Sept. 1750.

71 *DCt*, 5 Mar. 1751; *DWJ*, 9 Mar. 1751.

72 There was none for many months after those recorded in *DCt*, 5 Mar.; *DWJ*, 2, 9 Mar. 1751.

73 *DCt*, 27 July 1751.

74 *PO*, 27 Mar., 11 June 1751.

75 *PO*, 17 Aug; *DCt*, 30 July, 20 Aug.; *DWJ*, 2 Aug. 1751.

76 *DCt*, 9 July, 24, 28 Sept., 29 Oct.; *PO*, 6 July, 17, 24, 28 Sept., 1, 19, 29 Oct., 2, 5, 26 Nov. 1751.

77 *PO*, 18 Aug. 1752, 6 Feb. 1753.

78 *PO*, 14 May 1753.

79 *PO*, 21 Apr., 9 May 1752, 22 June, 16 July, 7 Sept 1754, 11 Nov. 1755; Gilbert (ed.), *Ancient records*, x, 134–5.

80 *DCt*, 31 Dec. 1751; *PO*, 16 Jan., 22, 29 May, 7 Aug. 1753; 11, 18 June, 9 July, 30 Nov. 1754.

81 *PO*, 14 Apr. 1753.

82 *PO*, 14 Apr. 1753, 16 Feb. 1754, 1 Apr., 16 Sept. 1755.

83 See, for example, *PO*, 20, 31 Aug. 1754, 31 May, 10 June, 15, 22 July 1755, 20 Apr. 1756.

84 *PO*, 24 May 1755.

85 *PO*, 26 Aug. 1755.

86 Hartington to Devonshire, 25 Aug. 1755 (PRONI, Chatsworth Papers, T3158/838).

87 *PO*, 14,17 June, 1, 15, 22, 26, 29 July, 9, 12 Aug., 16 Sept. 1755, 18 May, 29 June, 1756, 10 May 1757.

88 Gilbert (ed.), *Ancient records*, xi, 14.

89 S. Murphy, 'The Dublin anti-union riot of 3 December 1759' in G. O'Brien (ed.), *Parliament, politics and people* (Dublin, 1987), pp 49–68; J. Kelly, *Henry Flood: patriotism and politics in late eighteenth-century Ireland* (Dublin, 1998), pp 72–4.

90 *FJ*, 11 Aug. 1764.

91 This is elusive but some sidelights are provided on the process in *FJ*, 4, 18 Sept. 1764.

92 *DG*, 1 Nov. 1737, 30 Apr. 1765; *FJ*, 4 May, 30 July 1765.

93 *FJ*, 3 Aug. 1765.

94 *FJ*, 28 Apr. 1764.

95 *FJ*, 7 Dec. 1765, 1 Apr. 1766; *DM*, 4 Oct. 1766.

96 *FJ*, 12, 19 Dec. 1767, 3 Sept., 17 Dec. 1768, 28 Feb., 7 Mar., 24 June, 8 July 1769; *FLJ*, 26 Sept., 24 Oct. 1767.

97 *FJ*, 28 Apr. 1764, 5 Sept., 12 Dec. 1767, 3 Sept. 1768, 14 Jan. 1769; *DM*, 27 Dec. 1766.

98 *FJ*, 19 Dec. 1767, 14 Jan., 28 Feb., 7 Mar. 1769.

99 *FJ*, 24 June, 8 July 1769, 20 Sept. 1770; *FLJ*, 4 Aug. 1770.

3. THE CHANGING CHARACTER OF FACTIONAL DISORDER, 1770–95

1 *FJ*, 10 Oct. 1769, 17 Aug. 1779.

2 *FJ*, 31 Aug. 1773, 28, 31 Aug. 1790, 3 Sept. 1791; *HJ*, 1 Sept. 1780, 30 Aug. 1782, 27 Aug. 1784, 26, 28 Aug. 1789; *VEP*, 16 July 1785; *DC*, 19 Aug. 1788; S. Ó Maitiu, *The humours of Donnybrook: Dublin's famous fair and its suppression* (Dublin, 1995).

3 Gilbert (ed.), *Ancient records*, xii, 106, 137, 249–50; *HJ*, 25 July 1773; Waller to Macartney, 28 Aug. 1773 in Thomas Bartlett (ed.), *Macartney in Ireland, 1769–72* (Belfast [1978]), p. 169.

4 *FLJ*, 1 Aug. 1770; *FJ*, 19 Apr. 1774, 16 May 1778.

5 *FJ*, 27 July, 13 Aug. 1776; *FLJ*, 21 Aug. 1776.

6 *FLJ*, 21 July 1770; *HJ*, 5 Mar. 1773.

7 *FJ*, 27 July 1773, 13 May, 2 Sept. 1780; *HJ*, 12 Apr. 1776, 6 May 1789; *FLJ*, 17 Apr. 1779; T.J. Westropp, 'A glimpse of Trinity College', *Journal of the Royal Society of Antiquaries of Ireland* 18 (1887–8), p. 402.

8 N. Burton, *Letters from Harold's Cross* (Dublin, 1850), p. 40.

9 *HJ*, 15 May 1776, 7 May 1790; *FJ*, 19 May 1776.

10 *FJ*, 3 Aug. 1773, 21 Apr., 16 June 1774; *HJ*, 6 Aug., 8 Oct. 1773, 13 June 1774; *FLJ*, 22 June, 20 July 1774.

11 *FJ*, 4 May 1771, 28 Apr. 1774, 5 May 1798; *HJ*, 31 Mar., 3 May 1773, 1 May 1776.

12 *FJ*, 6 Nov. 1788, 20, 22 Oct. 1789, 18 Oct. 1791.

13 *HJ*, 2 Aug. 1771, 4 Aug. 1775, *FJ*, 6 May, 24 Aug. 1771, 3 Nov. 1778, 2 Jan. 1779, 30 Oct. 1787, 15 June 1790.

14 *FJ*, 26, 28 Aug., 20 Nov. 1779; J. Smyth, *The men of no property* (Basingstoke, 1992), pp 122–39.

15 *HJ*, 3, 15 Feb. 1775, 14 Aug. 1779; *FJ*, 24 Aug. 1775, 23, 28 Aug. 1781, 9 Apr. 1782; Morley, *Irish opinion and the American war*, pp 90–5, 127–9.

16 *HJ*, 12 Apr. 1786; *FJ*, 1 Feb. 1785, 31 May 1791.

17 *FJ*, 3 Sept.; *HJ*, 4 Sept. 1782.

18 J. Kelly, 'Parliamentary reform in Irish politics 1760–90' in David Dickson et al (eds), *The United Irishmen* (Dublin, 1993), pp 84–5; *FJ*, 16 Sept. 1784.

19 *DC*, 19 July 1787.

20 Orde to Pitt, 2 Aug. 1784 (Suffolk Record Office, Pretyman Papers, HA119/T108/34); S.H. Palmer, *Police and protest in England and Ireland, 1780–1850* (Cambridge, 1988).

21 Walsh, *Ireland sixty years ago*, pp 3–5.

22 *FJ*, 1, 3 Apr., 11 May, 5 June 1790.

23 *FJ*, 13 May; *DC*, 11, 13 May 1790.

24 *FJ*, 8, 10 June, 8 July, 3 Aug. 1790, 18, 21 June, 5 July, 18 Aug. 1791, 15, 25 Nov. 1792; *HJ*, 9, 11, 21 June 1790; *DC*, 8 July 1790.

CONCLUSION

1 In this context, the Irish experience is consistent with Alan McFarlane's observation of local history generally that the 'available data' allows the construction of 'events and actions rather than thoughts and feelings' (cited in Marshall, *The tyranny of the discrete*, p. 75).

2 *PO*, 8 May 1753; *FJ*, 28 Sept. 1765; Tuckey, *Cork remembrancer*, pp 140–1, 143, 151, 153, 160–1.

3 J. Kelly, *'That damn'd thing called honour': duelling in Ireland, 1570–1860* (Cork, 1995), p. 191ff.